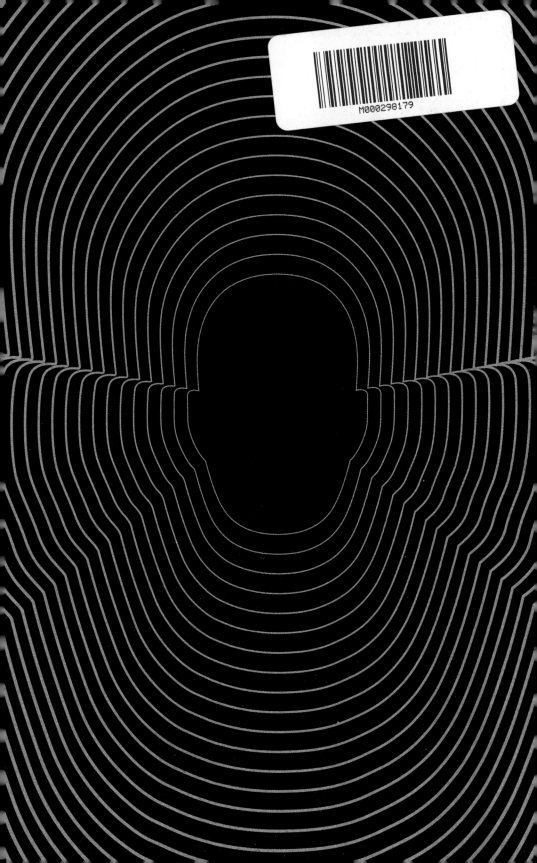

64 SHOTS

LEADERSHIP IN A CRAZY WORLD

KEVIN ROBERTS, CHAIRMAN, SAATCHI & SAATCHI

64 SHOTS

LEADERSHIP IN A CRAZY WORLD

KEVIN ROBERTS, CHAIRMAN, SAATCHI & SAATCHI

powerHouse Books
Brooklyn, NY

"Do not be concerned about the future;
keep your attention on today, and stay
in the present moment."

— *Don Miguel Ruiz*

CONTENTS

INTRODUCTION BY
KEVIN
ROBERTS

64 is a magic number.

Remember 1964? It was a landmark year that changed the world in many ways. The Beatles held the top five positions on *Billboard*, headed by "Can't Buy Me Love." Bob Dylan recorded "The Times They Are A-Changin'." The Rolling Stones released their first album. Dr. Martin Luther King, Jr. was awarded the Nobel Peace Prize and President Lyndon B. Johnson enacted the Civil Rights Act. Nelson Mandela gave his "I Am Prepared to Die" speech over three hours from the dock before being sentenced to 27 years. Cassius Clay became both heavyweight champion of the world and Muhammad Ali. BASIC computing language was introduced and the computer mouse was invented. Protests began against the Vietnam War. Andy Warhol began his most celebrated period.

1964—I was 15 years old…and hungry for life.

It turns out that 64 is a super-perfect number. The square root of 64 is the lucky number eight. There are 64 squares on a chessboard, and the *Karma Sutra* has 64 positions (but you know that!). Sixty-four is the country calling code for New Zealand, my home on the edge of the world. And the title of a famous Lennon and McCartney love song from the greatest album of all time.

This book *64 Shots*—a shot being a fast swing, an injection, a strong drink, an explosive charge, a Moon shot—is designed to help leaders succeed in today's ultra-turbulent world. I wrote it to bring a sense of optimism to a Volatile, Uncertain, Complex, and Ambiguous era. VUCA forces are eroding the ground under every organization and individual. Technology, in particular, has sparked an incredible moment. Industries, companies, and entire societies are being reset at record pace. Falling behind or getting ahead in life is an intense high-speed contest.

I have distilled 64 shots for leaders and aspiring leaders to meet today's extraordinary demands. Leadership is the defining difference in any field, and leading people in a crazy world requires a wider range of skills and emotional capabilities than ever. A leader's skillset has to be meta, macro, and micro; soft and hard; strategic and creative; directional and executional.

The book is inspired by Saatchi & Saatchi which is the central current in my business life. I spent 20 years as a client, then 17 years as Saatchi & Saatchi's global CEO, and one year as Executive Chairman, which evolved into Chairmanship. The *Lovemarks* book series was my means of reframing the industry I found myself in; leadership, however, is my passion.

These 64 shots assemble everything I've learned in business to propel the 21st-century leader. They are the basis of my operating style, teaching method, frameworks and formats, and forward focus. Their launch pad is the wisdom of a pantheon of leaders across fields and time.

In these crazy times, everyone must lead. My goal with *64 Shots* is to liberate you, the leader, from mind-numbing management literature. This book is meant to inspire, unleash, and entertain you. These 64 jabs to the solar plexus are quick sets of illumination, activation, and acceleration. Different shots will help different people. Go straight to what helps most, or read the book cover-to-cover for the full treatment on leadership. There is a linear logic to the shots but each set of four is a stand-alone idea.

Another meaning of "shot" is a photograph, an image, and the act of taking one. There are 64 shots in this book that form a parallel story, a book-within-a-book. These portraits are of people who have had a pervasive and inspirational impact on me. Some I know. They are all impact people. All are leaders who have "been through it." The book feels complete with them because I stand on their shoulders on my own leader's journey.

64 Shots comes from the worlds of business and sport. It is for anyone leading any group of people anywhere. I hope there is something here that will inspire you, and help you set others free.

And whatever you do, make sure you take the shot.

KR
New York
January 2016

CHAPTER — 01
THE FOUR AGREEMENTS

Years ago, Procter & Gamble's CEO A.G. Lafley sent me a book for Christmas. It was *The Four Agreements: A Practical Guide to Personal Freedom* by spiritual teacher Don Miguel Ruiz.

Every problem in business has its root cause somewhere in the Four Agreements. The genius is their simplicity: 1. Be Impeccable with Your Word, 2. Don't Take Anything Personally, 3. Don't Make Assumptions, 4. Always Do Your Best. The Four Agreements are bedrock. They underpin every word in this book.

Be Impeccable with Your Word

When I was 45, I had laser eye surgery because I couldn't handle glasses. I had eight pairs. I sat on them, broke them, lost them, and got totally frustrated. I found a surgery guy in New York, the best it seemed—he'd just done President Bill Clinton's eyes.

The procedure was simple. Fifteen seconds for each eye. "What is your success rate?" I asked. He said: "100 percent." I said: "Nonsense. No way can it be 100 percent. How?" The response:

– "I'm the best there is."
– "I've got the best equipment, come and have a look."
– "Before I agree to take you, you have to do eight weeks training in a test program. You're going to improve, build this muscle, that muscle…, so that by the time you get through that program, I'm 100 percent certain of success. Or I call it off."

I passed, it worked. A 100 percent record means a 100 percent record. Are you impeccable with your word? Think again; your pants are on fire.

Impeccable! Starting as kids, people tell white lies, fibs, porkies, or whoppers. We do this to save face, to get people off our back, to cover our ass.

"Impeccable" means do what you promise all the time, not almost all the time. It means unimpeachable, flawless, 100 percent. It means if you say "I'll call you back in 60 minutes," you do. The 61st minute is too late. Plans made were for a minus-60 minute response, the time frame on which you gave your word. Knock-on effects? The idea was murdered, the competition beat us, the crisis went global, the brand dissolved.

Be impeccable with your word. When I worked for Procter & Gamble in the Middle East, my boss Herbert Schmitz told me: "There are only two types of people in this world Kevin, those that deliver, and those that don't." That is being impeccable with your word. It's very hard to keep your word all the time, but every time people break their word it interrupts organizational Flow, and Flow sustains Peak Performance.

If you can't be impeccable with your word, don't give it.

Don't Take Anything Personally

Business is a blood sport. The key is to make sure it's not *your* blood. Bob Seelert brought me into Saatchi & Saatchi in 1997. Bob told me that to run the company effectively you needed, every morning, to "strap on a waterproof back and a bulletproof vest." Whenever the flak flew, it bounced off my front or ran off my back. I observed everything and acted when I needed to, but never got mortally wounded. I kept my ego in check, and my id intact. This way I maintained momentum, optimism, and conviction for 17 years as CEO.

The secret? Don't take anything personally. People take everything personally. Work is no exception. Countless projects are derailed by someone taking something personally. Check all egos, shoulder chips, and nerves at the door. It's not about whose idea it is, nor about whose business it is. It's about whose world it is. It's about what's best for the customer, the consumer, the fan. The fact that I may fiercely disagree with my team on what's best does not remotely change how I feel about them.

I always recoil when brand managers talk about "my brand." It is not their brand. It is their business, but the brand belongs to its customers. Coca-Cola executives got the memo in 1985, when they reformulated the original with "New Coke," and Coke customers poured the new concoction into the gutters of Atlanta.

Politics is mega-personal, a storm of conflicting personal agendas, distractions, frustrations, and conspiracies. In politics, either nothing gets done or it takes forever, thus ensuring maximum collateral damage. Business works faster. Great business stays focused on the audience, the idea, the issue, the facts, and the solution. You can't take stuff personally. If you do, you'll suffer. So will the outcome.

Don't Make Assumptions

Assumption is the mother of all #@%!-ups. An assumption is a fact taken for granted. We've all got those kinds of facts. Few facts are, in fact, incontrovertible. The American businessman Harold S. Geneen wrote about "unfactual facts." He talked about "accepted facts," "apparent facts," "assumed facts," "reported facts," and "hoped-for facts." Geneen demanded the "unshakable fact," a "genuine snapping turtle" of a fact. He urged management to "smell" a "real fact" from all others, and to do what it takes to be sure it is one.

Former U.S. Secretary of Defense Donald Rumsfeld talked about "known knowns," "known unknowns," and "unknown unknowns." Here is a rule of thumb: the less you assume, the more you explore, the better the outcome. Never assume; investigate. Be curious, pose questions, go to the source, and course correct.

This is *Genchi Genbutsu,* aka "Getcha boots on." It's a key part of the legendary Toyota Production System. It means go and see for yourself. Saatchi & Saatchi gets many insights through its Xploring research, where we observe people in their real day-to-day lives. If you want to understand how a tiger hunts, don't go to the zoo, go to the jungle. Toyota tracks back to the root of a problem through a process of asking "Why?" five times. No problem can sustain that kind of pressure. My three- and five-year-old grandchildren are masters of the art. No problem can sustain a child's "five whys."

To understand customers, you have to listen to them, watch them, smell them, touch them. Don't assume based on data. Data leads to false facts. Data reads the lines, but people live between them.

When iPod and iTunes came along, Sony had great facts on the Walkman. Sony interrogated the data, and knew just what people wanted. Multiple product improvements were on the way. People wanted this kind of Walkman and that kind. It was a fact. They had all the facts. Good luck reading all that. Goodbye Sony Walkman.

Harold S. Geenen said: "Facts from paper are not the same as facts from people. The reliability of the people giving you the facts is as important as the facts themselves." I was taught to interrogate the data. In my experience of this, either:

- – The group was not representative.
- – The wrong questions were asked.
- – It's been set up to elicit a pre-determined result.
- – The interviewer was a Muppet.
- – It won't play like this in Brussels.

I interpret the interpreters. I think "interrogate the data" means add your emotional quotient. Truth is in the grey, not the black-and-white. A leader listens to people's conclusions from "the facts." A leader looks at the topline data, minimizes assumptions, and decides on time—applying retired four-star general Colin Powell's 40/70 rule: "Use the formula P=40 to 70, in which P stands for the probability of success and the numbers indicate the percentage of information acquired. Once the information is in the 40 to 70 range, go with your gut."

And as Powell also said: "Don't let adverse facts stand in the way of a good decision."

Always Do Your Best

A major influence on my approach to leadership is American NFL coach Vince Lombardi. Lombardi demanded perfection knowing that it didn't exist. He knew the hearts of men. In 1959, the Green Bay Packers were coming off a 1-10-1 season, their ninth losing season in 11 years. Lombardi took command as head coach and general manager. With Lombardi, the Packers never had a losing season. It was 98-30-4 in nine seasons, including 9-1 in the postseason. Five championships, three straight, 1965-67. In 2000, ESPN named Vince Lombardi the "Coach of the Century." Vince Lombardi said this:

"Winning isn't everything, but wanting to win is."

Always do your best; this is very rare. Most of us do what's good enough, what's fit for purpose, what's appropriate, what will get by. But our best requires sweat equity, focus, commitment, and discipline. The challenge in front of us can demand that we not be tired, that we not go out the night before. It can demand we feel fit, on top of things, confident and full of self-esteem. Too often we don't meet the challenge head-on.

Our best means being in an area where we can grow. Most of us are forced into compromise by our bosses, husbands, wives, or children. We are dealt "a bad hand," so we don't always do our best. We do our best when it suits us. That's rubbish; capitulation.

Since day one, I've wanted to win. I try to do my best all of the time. Get yourself into a position where you do less and you play to your strengths with single-minded focus. This takes mental toughness.

SHOTS 01—04

Being average is a waste, and can get really boring. Being the best you can be, in your own mind, not in anybody else's, is a cool thing. It means you don't get frustrated, bitter, cynical, jealous, or regretful. If you know you're giving it all you can give, it simply feels great. No one can ask for more. You feel upbeat, positive, optimistic, and seriously happy. You win in life.

Always do your best. Give it everything, every time. Take it from Vince Lombardi:

"Winners never quit and quitters never win."

KEVIN ROBERTS

CHAPTER — 02

LIVING IN A VUCA WORLD

We live in a VUCA world. Volatile. Uncertain.
Complex. Ambiguous. VUCA is a military
acronym that has penetrated business speak.
It recognizes that running a business has become
like flying through an asteroid field.

IT'S A VOLATILE WORLD ALL RIGHT Market turmoil, currency swings, insurgencies, nature's fury, cultural uprisings, viral attacks, disappearing jobs, shareholder activism, consumer revolts. Not even the short list.

IT'S AN UNCERTAIN WORLD Equally fantastic or fatalistic, depending on your world view. No one has a clue what's around the corner. Every day, the corner gets closer. Tomorrow is in your face. Companies must reinvent, or die. In a 2015 *Fortune* survey of Fortune 500 CEOs, rapid technological change was the greatest threat. Ninety-four percent of respondents expected their companies to change more in the next five years than in the past five.

IT'S A COMPLEX WORLD Seven billion people need to have shelter, eat food, drink water, stay healthy, get along, be happy, pay for it all, keep the planet green, and fight off aliens. Not easy; totally doable. We will find the answers together.

IT'S AN AMBIGUOUS WORLD The world has overall become a better place, as key indices such as poverty levels show. However it's an obscure world with double edges. We're less hungry; more obese. We're connected, but distracted. Clear roads are hard to find.

Spears to rockets, was it ever not a VUCA world? The difference is that today VUCA travels wider, moves faster, and can hit harder than ever. People are saturated, cash-strapped, inundated with flak, and stressed by the pace of living. It's an Age of Now, a time of constant, instant far-flung impacts. People survive and thrive in the moment.

ERA OF NEW	AGE OF NOW
Analogue	**Digital**
High-speed	**Warp-speed**
Delayed impact	**Instant impact**
Low-tech	**Hi-tech**
Developmental	**Exponential**
Bounded world	**Boundless world**
Incremental	**Quantum**

"Controlling the controllables" is a myth in a moment world. There aren't many controllables, so don't spend a lot of time on that. I can't control my personnel cost ratio when it's pinned to revenue that can evaporate tomorrow. Marketers don't "own" the shopper. Consultancies don't "own" the client.

In a high-speed world, execution is hell. VUCA is random, brutal, and unforgiving. No matter what you just did today, no plan ever sustains first contact with the competition. No plan in a VUCA world ever survives 24 hours.

In this crazy future you need leaders. We need leaders more than ever. Leadership is teachable, and learnable. Everyone can be a leader, and Generation Next is up for it. The 2015 Deloitte Millennial Survey found that more than half (53 percent) of Millennials aspire to become the "leader or most senior executive within their current organization." In developed markets, this aspiration was 38 percent. In emerging markets, it was 65 percent.

By the time a problem lands on my desk, the black-and-whites are sorted. What's left is grey, hairy, and ugly. A leader is unequivocal. A leader decides, acts, and turns the tide. In 2010, in Jerusalem, I exchanged ideas with the statesman Shimon Peres, former Israeli President and Prime Minister, a leader of stature. He put it this way:

"A leader must decide. He says 'yes' or 'no.'"

Full stop.

LEADERSHIP ADVICE FROM A CONVERSATION WITH PRESIDENT SHIMON PERES IN JERUSALEM, OCTOBER 2010

Leaders must not be afraid of being alone.

They must have the courage to be afraid.

A leader must decide. He says "yes" or "no."

A leader must pioneer, not rule.

A leader is not on the top of his people
but ahead of them, in front.

Leadership is extremely hard work.

When you have chosen a destiny…never give up.

Leadership is based on a moral call.

What is right today is different tomorrow.

It's not enough to be up to date; you have to be up to tomorrow.

To lead is to listen, to pay attention to every detail, to decide.

Everything that once was controversial
ultimately becomes popular.

The more crazy life gets, the more decisive a leader needs to get. People laughed at U.S. President George W. Bush for saying, "I'm the decider, and I decide what's best." He was right. That is the job of a leader. A leader decides.

"To lead is to listen, to pay attention to every detail, to decide."

— Shimon Peres

Where should people start with "leadership" in a VUCA world? Leadership is both art and science. There are all kinds of leadership. There is not a one-size-fits-all approach. But the essence of leadership doesn't change. In the last 50 years, production, distribution, and communication have been reset by technology. Leadership hasn't changed much in 5,000 years. Technology doesn't alter leadership. It lets leaders reach more people, quicker, more emotionally—that's all. Leadership resists change because it's about human nature. Leaders take people to a better place.

My stance for leadership in a crazy world was inspired by some great leaders and coaches, notably Vince Lombardi and Peter Drucker, the man *Businessweek* said "invented management." Over 40 years, Drucker's straight-lefts seeped so gradually into my operating framework that I thought I'd invented them myself.

Drucker said: "Management is doing things right; leadership is doing the right things." In a VUCA world, doing things right is table stakes. Management is a science, driven by order, process, data, and digits.

Very important, but not the defining difference. This book is about doing the right things. And when things get crazy, leaders need to step forward.

As a platform, find leaders you can relate to. Study them. Learn from them. I study leaders who are winners. Lombardi used football to teach life. I try to do this through business.

Leadership is a question of character. It is a mix of qualities. Leaders know themselves and understand others. They show empathy and confidence. They decide when no one else has the guts.

You need your ABCs. Ambition. Belief. Courage. Avoid moderation. Good is no good. Aim to be a great leader. Greatness goes to extreme positions and makes extreme choices. A great leader stands for something transformational. Andy Warhol and Bob Dylan are two of my heroes. They led cultural transformational change. Warhol made art accessible in a remarkable way. Dylan transformed himself countless times and changed the way we think about the meaning of life. The great one, Steve Jobs, transcended both business and culture. He rode a rollercoaster of failure and success to change the way we live.

A leader is ready to go all in. Around 2004, I went all in with a question. Driven by fear of drowning in a flood of brands, I asked: what comes after brands? Power was shifting from brands to people. I could see the future beyond brands, I could feel it, force fields owned by people not corporations.

Love in business? Reactions were visceral. For creating the idea of Lovemarks, I got my fair share of mud pies. It was the sound of the ground breaking. Some said I was crazy when I wrote the book *Lovemarks: The Future Beyond Brands*. I am crazy. You should be too. As Oscar Wilde said:

"Nothing succeeds like excess."

10 PEARLS OF WISDOM FROM PETER DRUCKER

Management is doing things right;
leadership is doing the right things. 1

The only thing we know about the future
is that it will be different. 2

The best way to predict the future is to create it. 3

No institution can possibly survive if it needs geniuses
or supermen to manage it. It must be organized
in such a way as to be able to get along under a
leadership composed of average human beings. 4

People who don't take risks generally make about
two big mistakes a year. People who do take risks
generally make about two big mistakes a year. 5

Management by objective works—if you know the
objectives. Ninety percent of the time you don't. 6

Most of what we call management consists of making
it difficult for people to get their work done. 7

The most important thing in communication
is hearing what isn't said. 8

Making good decisions is a crucial skill at every level. 9

Plans are only good intentions unless they
immediately flow into hard work. 10

CHAPTER — 03

TURNING SUPERVUCA

"A pessimist sees the difficulty in every opportunity; an optimist sees the opportunity in every difficulty."

— Winston Churchill

I'm a radical optimist. In a VUCA world, you better be one. Getting down on your situation is the fastest way to lose. The T-shirt that says "nothing is as painful as regret" couldn't be more appropriate for today's world.

Everyone has to take responsibility for his or her own happiness. Indulging in guilt, worry, or regret creates massive barriers. This is self-indulgence. It uses up your bandwidth for happiness.

There's no room for negatives in business. No time for pessimists in a crazy world. People say "learn from the past." You can learn more from the present, and learn a lot more by anticipating the future. In a crazy world, hire radical optimists. Don't hire pessimists, contrarians, worriers, or cynics, except in fields where negative gearing has value. (Disaster avoidance, safety, security, insurance, prosecution, actually most of government springs to mind.)

Business is the world's positive gearing. It's our champion in a hi-tech time that is integrating everything. I have no fears of technology's dark side. We will manage this. The upside of the accelerator offers unparalleled potential for prosperity and harmony.

There are polar views on whether the hi-tech age will usher growth and well-being upwards and across. Much of this debate is wasted energy. The human elevator is not powered by science-led innovation. Nor is it powered by Disney-like imagination. Innovation and imagination are very important. The elevator, the magic lift, is in creativity. The unreasonable power of creativity drives growth. Creativity delivers the ultimate power in the universe, an idea.

"There is no doubt that creativity is the most important human resource of all. Without creativity, there would be no progress, and we would be forever repeating the same patterns."

—Edward de Bono

We live in the Age of the Idea. The potential to have an idea and, through technology, to distribute an idea, is unparalleled. "Creativity is just connecting things," said Steve Jobs. Ideas collide faster than ever. Ideas are biology. They can spin off, feed on, and kill each other at velocity. They will scale through the ricochet of objects, people, and systems.

Assemble all the bad news you like, and there's truckloads. It just leads to paralysis by analysis; stasis. We create the futures we believe in. I asked a group of 20-something students at the S.I. Newhouse School of Public Communications at Syracuse University what they thought "VUCA" means? Their response: Vibrant, Unreal, Crazy, Astounding. Welcome to the anti-VUCA, the SuperVUCA world.

IT IS A VIBRANT WORLD Dreams, hope, and optimism are shared at warp speed. The good thing is that "we are all incredibly alike where it matters," as an extreme traveler, Irishman Benny Lewis, put it. "Everyone just wants validation, love, security, enjoyment, and hopes for a better future." Connect what connects us, and everything changes.

IT IS AN UNREAL WORLD You used to need money, power, and scale to change the world. All you need today is an idea. At parity, you can't rationalize, process, or debate your way to glory. Ideas create Blue Oceans. Ideas are the currency of the millennium. The cultures with the most ideas, generated fastest, win.

IT IS A CRAZY WORLD Ideas are the most fragile things on earth. In most companies, the "Abominable No-Man," aided and abetted by cynics and contrarians, kills them at birth.

We need crazy people. Crazies are the only ones who will protect and nurture an idea. Crazies crack the case, nail the solution, score the goals, and win the game. Crazies are big-game players. It was crazy that Carli Lloyd scored a hat trick for the U.S. in the FIFA Women's World Cup 2015 final, scoring three goals in the first 16 minutes.

George Bernard Shaw said: "The reasonable man adapts himself to the world; the unreasonable one persists in trying to adapt the world

SHOTS 09—12

CLASSIC LEADER	CREATIVE LEADER
Team Leader	**Family Head**
On a Mission	**Has a Dream**
Paranoid Optimist	**Radical Optimist**
Rules-led	**Ideas-driven**
Instructional	**Inspirational**
Delegates	**Executes**

to himself. Therefore all progress depends on the unreasonable man." In a VUCA world, permission to misbehave is granted.

IT IS AN ASTOUNDING WORLD Technology connects people wherever they are. A good idea is worldwide in three hours. In Apple lingo: "Click. Boom. Amazing!" Tech is dissolving boundaries, switching out entire industries. Work/life integration is replacing work/life balance. Who leaves his or her job at work these days? We are living in an era of total integration.

In a crazy world, leadership evolves. Classic "command and control" leadership is dead in a high-speed world. SuperVUCA demands Creative Leadership. A leader today does two core things.

First, a leader creates other leaders. In business it is an imperative. Business leaders lead change, they lead transformation, and they do it through people. The fundamental role of the leader is to create more leaders; it's not about creating a great team.

I'm not a big believer in teams; a family will beat a team time after time after time. I like the silverback gorilla model. The outright leader encourages the young silverbacks to try him on. One day he gets flattened. He goes and sits in a tree with his wife, kids, and grandkids.

Bob Taylor, leader of the group at Xerox PARC, which designed the modern computer interface, said: "You can't pile together enough good people to make a great one." I believe that. It's so different to what they taught me at school. It's different to what every sports coach taught me. The group with the most great players will invariably win. In the 2015 Champions League football competition, Barcelona played Manchester City. The Blues, who I bleed support for, had one great player, Agüero. Barcelona had Messi, Neymar, and Suárez. Game over.

Under the Peter Principle, people are promoted to their level of incompetence. We've got to stop that nonsense. Hire the people you think have greatness inside them. Do it for every hire because you can't pile up enough good people to make one great one. Apply the test of Facebook Chairman and CEO Mark Zuckerberg:

" I will only hire someone to work directly for me if I would work for that person."

The second core thing that a leader does is inspire everyone they touch to be the best they can be—in pursuit of the company's purpose.

The leader has to make people the best they can be, not the best a leader wants them to be. If greatness is there, and in most groups it is latent, a leader will uncover it and unleash it. I try to inspire everyone I touch to discover and deliver their personal best. I listen aggressively, empathize, and bring out the best of a person based on what drives them.

In a high-speed world, the leader is also ideas-driven. The only way through VUCA is creative velocity, rapid-fire generation of ideas, ideas that are executed, ideas that win. The leader is in the field, knee-deep in the muck—inspiring others, testing ideas, deciding fast, and course correcting. The leader better be there, take joy in being there, and not pretend to be above it all. Otherwise it all stops.

The goal is a peak performing ideas group. Leadership is the ability to create other leaders, to inspire greatness, to unleash creativity, and to execute. In a VUCA world, what is right today is wrong tomorrow. In a SuperVUCA world, everyone must lead.

CHAPTER — 04

IT ALL STARTS WITH PURPOSE

Bob Isherwood—my creative partner at
Saatchi & Saatchi for many years—introduced
me to the Lewis Carroll line: "If you don't know
where you are going, any road will get you there."

I'm staggered by how many companies, brands, and people don't know where they are going. They have strategies and plans around the Yin-Yang, but are not driven by a purpose. Winning starts with purpose, is powered by it, is sustained by it. Saatchi & Saatchi's purpose has been core to my last 35 years (including my years as a client of the agency) and to the company's winning ways. Without that purpose we would never have survived the tumult of the mid-nineties.

To win in a crazy, upside down, and ever-changing world, the purpose must be clear and must be embraced by everyone. A leader must create the appetite for the relentless pursuit of purpose. This propels a team on a winning path. An organization with no purpose goes backwards in the Internet Age. Purpose creates belief, belonging, and direction. Purpose is why people work for you, buy from you, stay with you, share you, proliferate you. A purpose that is inspirational can take a business from 30mph to 300mph. In the digital era, it can globalize a company overnight. Yesterday's challenge for a business was to pump markets. The challenge in today's high-speed world is to create movements, and to inspire others to join in and accelerate its growth.

I've "purposed" people, brands, agencies, companies, teams, and countries. The platform is Peak Performance, a methodology developed with academic colleagues Mike Pratt, Clive Gilson, and Ed Weymes from the Waikato Management School, for getting to No.1 and—most importantly—staying there for over a decade, instead of rising and falling every few years.

SHOTS 13—16

PEAK PERFORMANCE PROGRESSION

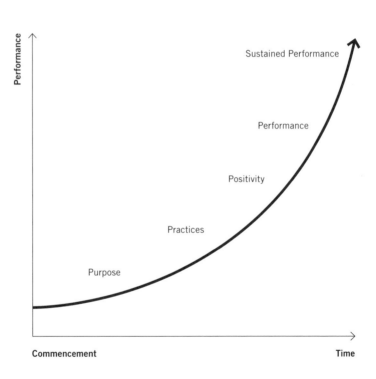

Most organizations have lots of rambling instead of purpose. They're fueled by generic platitudes that tick the stakeholder boxes. It's decoration. Dumbed-down banalities, meaningless dribble. Everyone swallows it. No one digests it. No one gets past the first sentence without nodding off or checking their email. The "purpose" gets posted to corporate Siberia, the "About Us" page. No one thumps the table when decisions threaten to run off course, saying, "This is what we stand for, this is who we are." I love Sol Kerzner's purpose: "To blow them away"—"them" being guests—that has fueled the growth of stellar experiences at my favorite One&Only resorts…Los Cabos Mexico being a great example.

Oliver Cromwell, British leader, soldier, politician, said: "My army won because they knew what they were fighting for and loved what they knew." Purposing has to start with the organization's leader. It can't be delegated. CEOs must take responsibility for their company having a brilliant purpose; nobody else. I'll only purpose a company if the CEO is side-by-side with me. The leader has to want to create it, to live it, to be present. Always. The global leadership team must co-create the purpose. It needs to inspire the next layer of leadership and cascade belief through the company for people to buy into, or to step out of.

The leadership team must generate the purpose itself. It must bring forth truth. In purposing an organization, I'll test, provoke, wrestle, cajole, and inspire the leadership group. In that situation, everybody stands up. The approach is caring and demanding. I care very much about the people and the outcome, and I try to inspire the team to feel the same way, and demand the maximum from each other.

The key to co-creating purpose is finding the right language. Revolution begins with language. When you find the right language, you change everything in an instant. Purpose demands emotional depth, because emotion leads to *action*. What is the idea that will unleash the organization? In every company, the right language is usually right there, just hidden, on the periphery. Purposing surfaces the language.

SHOTS 13—16

Generally speaking, it's the same story. The existing language is not aspirational enough, not provocative enough, not individual enough, not choiceful enough, and not colorful enough. I try to bring emotional resonance to the creation of purpose. What language captures and catalyzes the heart of this group? What is a choiceful, impactful, memorable set of words that provides clarity and meaning to everyone who comes into contact with it?

A leader leads with language. Shimon Peres in conversation with McKinsey: "Words are the connection between leaders and the public. They must be credible and clear and reflect a vision, not just a position. The three greatest leaders of the 20th century were Winston Churchill, Charles de Gaulle, and David Ben-Gurion. Each had a brilliant mind and a brilliant pen. Their ability with words demonstrated many things: curiosity, memory, courage. They understood that you lead not with bayonets but with language. A leader's words must be precise and totally committed."

In a crazy world, purpose is the framework for executional excellence. There are four foundations to a winning purpose in any enterprise.

Dream

I made the decision to join Saatchi & Saatchi in 1997 when this line rolled off my fax machine: "To be revered as a hothouse for world-changing ideas that transform our clients' businesses, brands, and reputations." My pulse raced. It was an Inspirational Dream, the most powerful force for change there is. The offer: to lead the most famous name in advertising.

How many organizations start each day with the rolling thunder of inspiration? Dr. Martin Luther King, Jr. did not say "I have a mission statement." He didn't talk about rules or tactics. He talked about a moral imperative, about the Promised Land. He had a dream.

Dreams are at the heart of all great endeavors. Dreams are immeasurable; they are about reaching for the stars, not counting them. President John F. Kennedy challenged Americans in the 1960s with the seemingly impossible dream: to put an American on the Moon and return him safely by the end of the decade. This dream set off a whole lot of planning, investment, hardcore science, endless experimentation. Without the dream all the practical stuff in the world doesn't add up to enough. In 1969, they got to the Moon, and back. Whether it's authentic or urban myth, the story of JFK visiting NASA headquarters in 1961 and asking a janitor what he did at NASA is apposite. The man replied, "I'm helping put a man on the Moon!" It's a variation on the architect Christopher Wren's visit to St. Paul's Cathedral in 1671 when he asked some of the stone masons: "What is your job here?" and among the replies came this diamond: "I'm building a Cathedral to the Almighty."

Extraordinary things happen when people have the guts to live their dream. The dream makes people want to belong and want to perform. A leader inspires people to be the best they can be in pursuit of a dream. The shared dream holds everything together and takes everyone higher. The dream must be present everywhere, in every conversation, filling the moment.

The Inspirational Dream expands the horizon of business possibilities to create the future. It is the touchstone for assessing all endeavors. And it enables the Greatest Imaginable Challenge: the most demanding and rewarding achievement that can be imagined within three to five years. Exciting, stimulating, stretchy, measurable. The Challenge is the Inspirational Dream in action.

Spirit

What is your vital emotional energizing principle? Purpose is fueled by Spirit. It is the DNA, the life-force of the organization, the flame burning in every person who is part of that organization.

Spirit is the magnetic power that harmonizes. Spirit defines character. The Spirit ladder is a set of attributes climbing towards the Spirit statement. The top rung is how you manifest externally.

CREATING IMPOSSIBLE IDEAS AT SAATCHI & SAATCHI

They said it couldn't be done	1
Through the eyes of a child	2
Out of the blue	3
Biting off more than you can chew	4
Pushing boundaries	5
Impossible dreams	6
Perpetual optimism	7
Messy logic	8
Refusing to accept defeat	9
Beyond comprehension	10

The core of Saatchi & Saatchi's Spirit is "Nothing Is Impossible," the essence of the buccaneering tonality of the company's founders, brothers Charles and Maurice Saatchi, back in 1970 in London. These three words are our most powerful recruiting tool. Who wouldn't want to sign up to this?! Nothing Is Impossible is neither an invitation to be reckless, nor is it just focused on meeting extreme requirements of clients. It is more than a business code and an operating method. It's a worldview. For me, it goes to the heart of leadership in a crazy world, where the winning operating system is radical optimism.

Beliefs

If you stand for nothing, you fall for everything. What do you believe in?

An organization's Beliefs explain why it creates sustainable value for its audiences. There should be eight aspirational and inspirational Beliefs about why it creates value. The Beliefs of a business should relate directly to the customer or consumer.

Belief creates culture, and culture eats strategy for breakfast. Belief is indestructible. Belief is very hard to defeat. It enables sustained Peak Performance.

The New Zealand national rugby union team, the All Blacks, epitomize Peak Performance. They are considered the most successful elite sports team anywhere, ever. Their dominance in international rugby is crushing.

How do you achieve a win-rate of 78 percent across 112 years? No rival is close to that. In the 54-Test period between winning the 2011 and the 2015 Rugby World Cups, the win-rate was over 90 percent.

The All Blacks believe that legacy is more intimidating than any opposition. When you play New Zealand you play against all the legends who wore that jersey, and you play against those standards. Jonah Lomu, one of the greats, said it was like putting an "S" on his chest front, as Mike Catt discovered in the World Cup semi-final of 1995 in

THE MIGHTY ALL BLACKS

Won 78 percent of games over 112 years.

Ranked No.1 for 10 of the 12 years since rankings began in 2003, including the last six years.

Between winning the 2011 and 2015 Rugby World Cups (RWC), played 54 Tests with a record of 49 wins, three defeats and two draws.

First team to defend a RWC.

First team to win three RWCs.

Only team to have never lost a RWC pool match.

Upon reaching 300 tries scored at RWCs, the next team was 100+ tries behind.

Cape Town. Jonah touched the ball just seven times, scored four tries, and created two more. Rugby doesn't get any better than that.

Between 2004 and 2011, the All Blacks' win-rate went to 86 percent. This has everything to do with culture and Beliefs. Among the All Blacks' system of Beliefs:

- Sweep the sheds: no one is too important to do the small things.
- Follow the spearhead: its force must move in one direction.
- "No Dickheads."
- Champions do extra; find ways to do more.
- Keep a blue head, stay on task, calm, and maintain clarity.
- Be a good ancestor; an All Black leaves the jersey in a better place.

For more depth on All Black leadership, see: *Legacy: 15 Lessons in Leadership: What the All Blacks Can Teach Us About the Business of Life* by James Kerr.

Amazon is another organization with powerful Beliefs. Jeff Bezos, founder and CEO, is "purpose-inspired." Amazon is obsessed with the customer. Amazon plays the long game. Don't bet against the thousand-yard stare of Bezos: "Take a long-term view, and the interests of customers and shareholders align."

Focus

Most companies have little or no focus. They have claptrap, applesauce everywhere, so nothing gets executed. Focus is the fundamental principle of thought and action. Saatchi & Saatchi's Focus: To fill the world with Lovemarks.

Focus is the point of origin from which business ideas and influences emanate. It explains how the organization delivers value every day, every hour, every second. Focus aligns everyday actions to deliver the organization's Greatest Imaginable Challenge. It determines direction and priorities. It enables everyone to understand how they contribute.

SHOTS 13—16

A Focus must be powerful, progressive, memorable, internal, and external. It should be action-based, starting with a verb. I was trustee of two Team New Zealand America's Cup challenges. Team New Zealand had this Focus: Make the boat go faster. That is Focus.

A Note on Personal Purpose

Every company needs a purpose on a page. I believe every individual needs this too. Winners observe the Delphic maxim "First, know thyself." Most people don't, and suffer for it. Ninety-nine percent of people don't have a defined personal purpose. They drift along in a canoe of compromise, aimless, effectively lost.

"I want to be rich." "I want to get my golf handicap down to five." "I want to retire when I'm 40." These are not dreams. It's pretend dreaming. It's settling for average, trucking down a pathway of balance and compromise. Human potential is precious. What are we here for, just to live and die?

What is your Inspirational Dream? What are the eight things you believe that nobody else does and nobody knows about that dictate your entire life? What is your Spirit, your Character, your Focus? In a single word, what is the defining quality of you?

We don't know ourselves because society teaches us not to. "Put family first." "Do it for the team." "Do it for the country." No, do it for yourself first. They say in business you have to promote three things: your boss, your subordinate, and the business. Nonsense. Look after yourself in there. Otherwise you're going to be a passenger. If you want to wear the captain's black armband, wear it, and be a great captain.

To get to Peak Performance, personal purpose and organizational purpose must align. If there are significant disconnects between them, people need to consider changing their role in the organization, reconsider their personal purpose, change the organization (hard!), or leave. Leading and winning, it all starts with purpose. As Vince Lombardi said:

JEFF BEZOS'S TOP 10 LEADERSHIP LESSONS

Base your strategy on things that won't change.	1
Obsess over customers.	2
We are willing to be misunderstood for long periods of time.	3
There are two kinds of companies: those that try to charge more, and those that work to charge less. We will be the second.	4
Determine what your customers need, and work backwards.	5
Our culture is friendly and intense, but if push comes to shove, we'll settle for intense.	6
If you want to be inventive, you have to be willing to fail.	7
In the old world, you devoted 30 percent of your time to building a great service and 70 percent of your time to shouting about it. In the new world, that inverts.	8
Everyone has to be able to work in a call center.	9
This is Day 1 for the Internet. We still have so much to learn.	10

SHOTS 13—16

Forbes, "Jeff Bezos's Top 10 Leadership Lessons," by George Anders, April 23, 2012.

"Only by knowing yourself can you become an effective leader."

Know yourself, and know when to change yourself. Companies should repurpose every decade, every time they make a big acquisition, and every time they switch businesses.

For individuals, repurposing is similar to organizations. People define themselves by the decade, so review the dream every 10 years. Character, Spirit, Beliefs, Challenge, and Focus won't change dramatically past 30 years of age. Tune them, adjust the weighting as needed.

My belief system is centered around Making Happy Choices. It's about meaning, not means. I don't like wearing a tie so I don't. I don't like playing golf or having business dinners, so I won't. I only break bread and drink wine with close friends and family. These days, I do stuff I love with people that I like in places I enjoy.

I love to teach business to young people. I believe business is a force for good. Business meets needs, solves problems, innovates, improves lives, builds self-esteem, creates jobs, and offers everyday joy. Jack Welch thought the role of business is to create shareholder value. Peter Drucker said it is to create and grow a customer. Both are half right. The role of business is to make the world a better place for everyone.

My personal purpose is *To make the world a better place through business*. I can only do that through people. Inspiration out is a direct factor of inspiration in, and young people inspire me.

STARTING UP PERSONAL PURPOSE: ASK FOUR QUESTIONS

What is my One-Word Equity?	1
When am I at my best?	2
What will I never do?	3
What is my five-year dream?	4

SHOTS 13—16

CHAPTER — 05

UNLEASHING EMPLOYEE ENGAGEMENT

Business isn't rocket science, though it does run on rocket fuel. Leaders must inspire people to be the best they can be in pursuit of a dream. Leaders inspire people towards greatness. They accelerate people beyond being good. They develop greatness in people through the four pillars: Responsibility, Learning, Recognition, and Joy.

I received all four early on in my career. I joined Procter & Gamble in 1975. P&G hired university graduates and promoted from within. I was a black sheep, checking neither box. I'd been kicked out of school when I was 17 years old. I knocked on P&G's door as a non-graduate inculcated with two work cultures: the creative velocity of Mary Quant, a hothouse of miniskirts, hot pants, and make-up to make love in; and Gillette, where I marketed women's toiletries and became a Mach 3 Turbo junkie. I spoke a couple of languages, knew how to sell, and being a rugby fly-half, was fast on my feet.

My educational quotient wasn't on P&G's charts. My emotional quotient was off them. In my mid-20s, I was faster, tougher, more aggressive than my peers, though not smarter. I needed training, and I persuaded P&G to make a recruitment exception. (Thank you Christian von Stieglitz.)

I started at the bottom, and got truckloads of learning. I rose up on the four pillars. Herbert Schmitz was a boss who unleashed me through responsibility, learning, recognition, and joy. He said: "Kevin, go fix Procter & Gamble in the United Arab Emirates and don't tell me what you did. Just give me results. Here are the five things I would do. The most important is get out of your office and get into the souks." He promoted me twice when nobody else would have gone near me.

SHOTS 17—20

He made it fun, not least because he introduced me to very good German wine. I performed through the roof for him.

The four pillars create a winning culture. Here are the fantastic four.

Responsibility

"The price of greatness is responsibility," said Winston Churchill. To lead is to take on responsibility, and every young person I meet wants a piece of that action.

Responsibility is the foundation. The key is to give people responsibility before they are ready. Spread every eagle's wings, unleash their potential, and extend their range. They will reward you beyond measure. I often get asked: "How do you retain talent?" Great people stay in places where they can do great work, their best work. It's as simple as that.

Responsibility has to be distributed because the further up a company you go, the more stupid you become, in rarefied air, enmeshed in strategy, and detached from what really matters. A leader creates leaders at every level of the company. A leader gives the decision to those closest to the action. Twenty-first century business happens in real time. Fail to devolve responsibility in the Internet Age, and you're gone.

Responsibility means taking ownership. It also means taking action. "The truth of the matter is that you always know the right thing to do. The hard part is doing it," said the Persian Gulf War General, Stormin' Norman Schwarzkopf. On a ranch in Arizona, he also gave me one of the best pieces of advice I've ever received: "When given command, take charge and do what's right."

A leader bears the scar tissue of responsibility. Leaders have been through it. They have emerged bloodied, but stronger. Nothing beats the feeling of the good fight and the great win. NFL coach Vince Lombardi:

"I firmly believe that any man's finest hour, the greatest fulfillment of all that he holds dear, is that moment when he has worked his heart out in a good cause and lies exhausted on the field of battle—victorious."

SHOTS 17—20

Learning

Elevated responsibility should take place in a framework of learning. Screwing up is OK, if you fix failure fast and learn from it.

Train people to do what they love, the activities they were born for. Play people in positions where they're at their best. I'm at my best when I'm the captain. In my first game of rugby, I was the youngest on the team. At half time, the coach made me captain. Today I'm at my best as a coach or mentor, but in operational situations, even if I'm not the designated boss in a group, I just assume command.

Established organizations usually provide responsibility and learning better than startups. Startups tend to fail constantly, without learning. Too often, responsibility rests with the founders and no one else has any responsibility. The founders ultimately wander into the land of the Peter Principle. As they reach their level of incompetence, it's time to sell.

Recognition

Recognition means giving people what they care about. Few companies do. Money is only important when you don't have any. It's a way of keeping score if you're insecure. Beyond a good amount it doesn't matter, unless you're a psycho banker who counts success by the number of zeros in your annual bonus and SEC fines dodged.

Give people money, and they're happy for three days. Then they think "I should have got more than that," "Joe makes more than me," or, "They've been screwing me for years obviously."

Money is table stakes, and someone will always pay more. Offer people value for value, and stop there. As an employer, I never counter-offer. I wish people well and let them know if it doesn't work out, to come back. And they come back, bunches of them.

Recognition programs are generally useless. As soon as you put a program behind recognition, it becomes an entitlement. What is real recognition? It's one-on-one. It's beyond personal. It's intimate. Ask this:

"What empathetic gesture will rock this overachiever's world?"

It's always different. It depends on the situation, the person. It could be an experience beyond reach, country relocation, spouse-synced vacation time, bringing children to work, tickets to a World Cup final. It might be a personal phone call on a job well done.

Recognize people personally, individually, and not just financially. Base it on who they are, not just what they did. They will perform better, stay longer, and take you higher.

Joy

The corporate world is potted with oppressive cultures, regimented hours, sterilized environments, toxic bosses, old boys' networks, penguin suits, and pet prohibition.

Research shows that the majority of employees are not engaged at work. It also shows happy people are more productive at work. Joy in the workplace is scant, yet its flow is critical. Happy people work harder than unhappy people. Happy people make other people happier. Business, especially service business, succeeds and wins on happiness and joy.

A winning culture is demanding, but not dispiriting. Its performance-driven engine hums with passion, harmony, and joy. My mission in life has been to emotionalize every enterprise I come in contact with. I rev the company engine and juice every driver on the grid. I've always liked business leaders who inject passion. Renzo Rosso at Diesel. Akio Toyoda at Toyota. My first boss, Mary Quant, a force of nature.

Instilling joy in work is the next big thing. Winning companies will empower people—as Oprah says—to live their best life every day. I don't mean work/life balance. I don't believe in it. I'm fundamentally opposed to balance in every shape and form. I believe that balance and moderation should be avoided at all costs.

The future is about work/life integration, creating conditions to harmonize the different realms of our lives to avoid trade-offs. It's about

SHOTS 17—20

finding ways to be the best you can be in everything—the best friend, the best partner, the best parent, the best business person, the best you! This creates sheer joy and fulfillment. The outcome is greater productivity.

The point is that to create a culture where ideas and innovation flow, you need all four pillars in equal parts, every day, upwards, downwards, and sideways. It can't be responsibility and learning this year and recognition and joy the next. Startups fall down on responsibility and learning. Established organizations fail on recognition and bomb joy.

All four factors must be given in the same time frame, in equal measure. People perform better when they know what the plan is, have responsibility to action it, someone's shown them how to do it, they're recognized for their ability to perform, and they have a spring in their step.

Leaders inject all four pillars into every conversation. They are disciplined in framing the conversation towards giving someone responsibility, encouraging them with a bit of learning, recognizing them, and letting them leave smiling. Unfortunately, caning someone—or constructive criticism (what an oxymoron!)—is still by far the most used management technique.

The four pillars are not just a boss-to-subordinate thing. If you don't give the four to your boss, why should she give them to you? Who inspires the inspirers? Who coaches the coach? Individuals have to give the pillars to their bosses, to their subordinates and to their peers. Networks beat hierarchies. Inspire horizontally and diagonally, not just vertically. Energy must build in all directions.

To create a winning culture, live and give these four pillars at all times. People will peak perform. Greatness will materialize. Ideas and innovation will flow.

SHOTS 17—20

CHAPTER — 06

RUNNING THE BUSINESS— THE 4 P'S

Every business, no matter the size, should be run on the 4 P's: Purpose, Performance, Product, and People. All four wheels must be aligned, spinning, and accelerating to sustain growth.

Peter Drucker said: "Meetings are by definition a concession to deficient organization. For one either meets or one works." I'm on board with this. Most meetings go off track, go on endlessly, the agenda is overstuffed with irrelevant rubbish to avoid talking about the real opportunities and issues at hand. Usually there is huge waste in terms of the preparation and execution around key meetings. Mountains of reports get circulated. And they go on far too long. Day-to-day meetings should be done in about 18 minutes, the time of a TED talk.

There are different types of meetings a company has during a year—the annual rally, the quarterly town hall, the regional heads pow-wow, the weekly work-in-progress. I only attend one: the monthly operational meeting. This is the meeting that runs the business. It is my "kitchen cabinet" meeting, a term that first came into vogue in the 1830s during the Presidency of Andrew Jackson. There was the formal "parlor cabinet," which was riven with controversy and dissent, and there was the "kitchen cabinet"—Jackson's group of trusted advisers—where the real work got done.

These meetings are structured precisely around the 4 P's. Who is in this meeting? The CEO obviously; where the buck stops. Then the three critical functions: operations, finance, and talent. We meet behind closed doors over a working lunch. We adhere strictly to format. No guests. No interruptions.

There is no leader/subordinate vibe in this meeting. The focus is on truth, not detail, explanations, or prevarication. I am not trying to prove anyone wrong, I just want the truth, no matter how ugly it turns out to be. There are no politics, no chit chat, no baggage, no confrontations, no chewing outs. The people in this group are there because they totally support each other. Everyone wants to be there. These are people I care about. The operating principles are the Four Agreements of Don Miguel Ruiz in action: be impeccable with your word; don't take anything personally; don't make assumptions; always do your best.

At the conclusion, there are no minutes or action lists issued. People know the things for which they take responsibility. This is what leaders do. Plus, I have an elephant's memory.

The 4 P's work for any company regardless of size. They are a simple, clear structure that anyone can follow. Drucker again: "No institution can possibly survive if it needs geniuses or supermen to manage it. It must be organized in such a way as to be able to get along under a leadership composed of average human beings."

Practice the 4 P's for success; ignore them at your peril.

Purpose

Every monthly operational meeting should start with reviewing progress against the business's purpose-on-a-page. It's a litmus test. Are we reaching for the dream, breathing our spirit, living our beliefs, showing our character, driving our focus, and progressing towards our Greatest Imaginable Challenge? How are our actions measuring up against the company purpose?

The shape of the purpose discussion is unpredictable because you are starting at the highest level. There is no telling what will get thrown up, and that's a good thing. Purpose is the stimulus for story sharing, anecdotes, insights, and examples. At the start of the meeting I want illumination and provocation, not analysis and detail. Before the crunch, check the view from space. Get a helicopter view of where you are. Then you can see where you need to go.

Performance

Winston Churchill would send memos under "Action This Day." A Churchill request would read: "Pray let me know by 4 P.M. today on one sheet of paper…"

No kitchen cabinet report should be longer than a page. Busy people need an efficient reporting system. So measure what matters and report what is critical. There are only three key performance indicators I care about: revenue, personnel costs, and margin. I want the story of these three KPIs on one page: how we are performing vs competition, commitment, and last year; ups and downs; and actions.

This is perfect process. But what if the content is soft, if a number is off? How long is patience? In my book, patience extends to 100 days. Put a 100-day plan around a problem, and fix it. Sometimes, the problem is just too big. Pierre Berbizier, who played scrumhalf for France, and captained and coached the team, would say:

"Don't just do things better; do things different."

If your growth stalls—and business is a growth game—you need to do something different—not just tweak or tinker. You may have to invest, buy, sell, merge, or disrupt your way out of trouble. There is a time to keep climbing upwards, and there is a time to find a way round. A time to reap. A time to sow.

Woody Allen's character in *Annie Hall,* Alvy Singer, nailed relationships. "It has to constantly move forward or it dies." The same applies to business.

Product

Product is where the rubber hits the road. It's what you make and sell. If you're in the shoe business you look at the new shoes: the shape, the heel, the color, the toe, the sole, the strap. How it fits with the season, the trends, the tastes of the times. At Saatchi & Saatchi we look at the work across the top 10 clients, top 20 geographies, work in development, work just made. We'll look at work that has won awards, work that has delivered outstanding results, and work that is innovative.

Most of the work that reaches the kitchen cabinet are not ads, they are ideas bigger than ads. At our last meeting we viewed a sensory exhibition for a camera, an interactive app for children's eyesight testing, an online game, a product design for a bank, a sponsorship case for a football club, a gratitude program for an auto brand, a mobile telecommunications innovation for Outback emergencies, two short documentaries (one about a lion having dental surgery, the other about a man shaving his 14-year-old beard and revealing his face for the first time to his wife and daughter), a magazine printed with blood for HIV awareness, and something that was described as "half stunt, half anthropological experiment" (naturally it was from Argentina).

Boy, life can be fun.

Regardless of what your product is, a winning company understands how an industry works, what customers want, and what competitors might do—and how these might change and be disrupted. You have to be immersed physically and intellectually in the product. Know, see, touch, feel, fondle; kick it and lick it. Be it. You can't run the business if you don't understand your product through and through.

People

It's fundamental that a group of happy people will outperform a group of unhappy people. The people part of the operational meeting is structured around the four pillars that inspire people on the job: responsibility, learning, recognition, and joy. You can't get eagles to fly in formation, but you can point them towards the open sky.

Within these four pillars are threaded a bunch of functional items. Top responsibility decisions: moves, promotions, assignments, issues, gaps to fill, are the right people in the right positions? How are the top 50 people tracking? The learning elements look at needs around both hard and soft skills as the industry moves at helter-skelter pace, at program effectiveness, and ways to infuse learning as an everyday opportunity. Recognition centers on salary decisions and other credits to be made.

And joy. The joy element is more about stories, anecdotes, and atmosphere. Is the joy factor going up or down in the organization? Are we doing enough? And are we feeling it personally?

There is a fifth P and it is invisible. It's the plumbing, and all good plumbing should flow seamlessly, work every time, at every flush or turn of the tap. Water should appear when needed, and be otherwise absent. Our Chief Operating Officer is "The Master Plumber." He keeps people and their teams in the Flow zone; clears blockages and makes connections. Our COO: "I'm proud of being The Plumber. My job is all about flow. Plumbers build things to flow, and they fix things when they aren't flowing properly. I help people and teams work in flow because that is where our ideas are created and delivered. From this flows revenue and growth."

Every organization needs someone to be The Plumber, an operations ace who handles blockages and potential blockages. Plumbing problems need to be handled before the monthly meeting.

A WINNING COMPANY

Driven by Leaders

Very high performance aspirations held by all key leaders.

Demanding, "unreasonable" CEOs.

Effective working group at the top.

Ability to penetrate to micro-level of their businesses.

Single-minded adherence to clear success measures.

Built by Relentless Pursuit of Purpose

Highly motivating Purpose.

Oriented around leadership and growth.

Consistently strive for both profitability and growth.

Passionate defenders of core businesses.

Understand how industry works, what customers want, and what competitors can do—and how these might change.

Simple Structures and Core Processes

Straightforward alignment of authority, accountability, and performance challenges (RASC).

Uncomplicated lines of communication and approval.

Energized by Intense Performance-Driven Culture

Demanding, occasionally punishing, work pace.

Real follow-through on accountability—especially at the top.

Fail Fast, Learn Fast, Fix Fast.

"Good" place to work—not always "nice."

Performance shortfalls change careers.

Based on World-Class Skills

Do many things well, but at least one functional skill—at world-class competence level—underpins success.

Key management processes viewed as real competitive advantage.

Rejuvenated by Well-Developed People Systems

CEO is Chief Personnel Officer.

Clear focus on performance and motivation.

Four pillars—Responsibility, Learning, Recognition, and Joy.

SHOTS 21—24

CHAPTER — 07

MAKING THINGS HAPPEN

When I joined Saatchi & Saatchi in 1997, the agency was riding low in the water. The company was demoralized, losing money and clients, and was crippled with debt. I came on deck as captain. I brought both continuity and change.

The fame and mystique of the agency was down to the Saatchi brothers, its founders. Applying the first rule of change management, I was clear what should not change:

- The "Nothing Is Impossible" mantra.
- The practice of only hiring passionate, competitive, restless people.
- The belief in and focus on the work, the creative product.

Righting the boat would require audacity, inspiration, and a measure of foresight. I reframed the advertising agency as an "Ideas Company." We added "One Team, One Dream" to "Nothing Is Impossible." I also got rid of the legal department. No lawyers, no legal problems.

We focused on the top-line not the bottom, on the work not the process, on performance not promises, on employees not shareholders, on teamwork not individuals, on infatuating existing built-to-last clients, not the chasing of specious new business.

Together, we were up and running. Now for acceleration. Once you have purpose, you need results. American writer Gina Trapani wrote something great on productivity: "Getting things done is not the same as making things happen." To make things happen, I brought RASCI into Saatchi & Saatchi.

RASCI makes things happen. RASCI is a superb project management tool. It attacks the complexity of a crazy world by assigning accountabilities. It's an acronym that stands for Responsible, Approve, Support, Consult, and Inform.

SHOTS 25—28

The beauty of the system is its non-hierarchal role clarity. Anybody can play in any position, regardless of title. Of course, who should play where is often obvious.

At the outset of any initiative, roles are assigned. The project typically has one person responsible and one approver. Others on the team are designated as either an S to do the support work, a C to be consulted, or an I to be informed.

Embedding this approach is a way to remove silos, confusion, duplication, and waste. There is total accountability for every project and every decision. Relationships for a project are established and clear. Whether a project is local or global, it is clear who does what with whom. Teamwork is fostered. Creativity is enhanced, providing more time for what's important. The result is Flow.

RASCI is well known and widely used. I call it RASC not RASCI. Informing the "need to knows" is obvious. And "I" can quickly stand for interference.

R-esponsible
A-pprove
S-upport
C-onsult

The RASC idea has variations, so there are different acronyms for it. What's interesting is how almost all companies butcher the roles of Responsible, Approve, Support, and Consult. The result is a monkey house: C-onsult, R-esponsible, A-pprove, P-rop.

Here are the RASC roles, along with common mistakes that people make when executing. These are the games people play.

Responsible

The R is responsible for driving the project to completion. The R is pivotal. Success depends on the R.

The biggest problem with RASC is that most people revert to hierarchy—but the whole point of RASC is that it's non-hierarchal. Most people scupper RASC. We all write RASC. We all teach it. Nobody uses it. The point is to have dynamic role fulfillment, not a chain of command.

Robert Senior, who succeeded me as Saatchi & Saatchi global CEO, talks about "playing in position." This is what RASC means. The right person plays and stays in the right role. It doesn't mean "kick it back up to the boss" or "kick it to the sideline."

When a project or budget or challenge arises, the first question to ask is: "Who is responsible for running this?" Usually the busy line leaders will put their hands up. "It's my responsibility. I have the P&L, I know the client..." Wrong. The R should be the person with the biggest vested interest and the most skills and the most passion to see the project through. This is never the hierarchical leader. The hierarchical leader is usually busy and doesn't have the passion, drive, or time to put against this particular project. The ball gets played out of position. The game is lost.

The whole point of RASC is to get decision-making passed down the organization. The closer it is to clients, customers, and fans, the more you win. Instead, people fall back on hierarchy and job titles. The cogs stop turning. The machine grinds to a halt.

SHOTS 25—28

Approve

The A has final signoff on the delivered project. Mistakenly, people think the approver is ahead of the R in the hierarchy and is there solely to decide. The true role of the A is to coach, guide, and inspire the R to make the right decision, and then to approve the resources.

The relationship between the R and the A is a conversation. It is not a memo sent up the pipe for a rubber stamp. It is not judgment day. The A has the responsibility to help the R get the right result. The A has bought into the task. The A has a nurturing role throughout. Otherwise, the A shouldn't be on the project.

The A role can be described as "Accountable." The A must take accountability. Approval is the tip of the A iceberg.

Support

The S role is pretty straightforward. An S sweats bullets for the R in the day to day. S people do the actual work. An S gets it done, making it happen for the R.

Failure to delegate tasks can make life hard. Delegation is something my children have learned. They all knew RASC from a young age.

The great thing about RASC is that it works everywhere. It can be used in professional or personal situations. Take it on your family vacation. "Who's responsible for the food?" "Who is going to transport it?" "Who knows where to get fresh strawberries, grandma's favorite thing in the world?" "Who is accountable if there is death by chocolate?"

When there is no clear RASC, we don't get into Flow zones. Mayhem ensues. People don't know if they are the R, the A, the S, or the C.

Consult

A consult is someone who an R can call on to give advice. It's a word from the wise. Being a C is the best of all worlds. Stroke your chin, dispense wisdom, and then let the R do what's right. I prefer to be a C to an A, and tend not to take the R role now. If I take an R it's to unravel a Gordian knot, and I want an experienced or resourceful person as the A.

At Saatchi & Saatchi, we consult people who have a vested interest in the outcome or whose experience can provide value to the project. The mistake that people make with the C is time. So we set it up thus: "We'll give you 48 hours to give us your advice. We'll listen hard, but that's all. If the R ignores your advice, deal with it. It's one team, one dream."

The 48-hour rule heads Machiavelli off at the pass. What you don't want, and what usually happens, is politicking, undermining, litigation after the fact, and the most destructive phrase in corporate life, "but no one kept me in the loop." If you're not in the RASC loop, you're not meant to be, and don't let it concern you.

Making Things Happen

How to embed RASC? Educate people. I won't give up because people don't get it. To bake RASC in, I try to demonstrate. So the question I ask on any issue is: "Who's got the R?" In ideal situations, I don't even have to ask because the enthusiast in the room has his or her hand up saying, "I'm the R."

And ideally, again, the R should be able to deal with his or her own A, S, and C. Who do I call? I don't want to call the boss or the boss's boss. The boss won't have the answer. The boss will have to stop work. This is unhelpful. The boss will call one of his or her people who will also have to stop work. This is also unhelpful. I'll call the R, stop all that, and get the right answer immediately.

Practice, practice, practice. Lead by example. Lead by doing. If the CEO keeps putting his or her hand up and saying "it's my decision," the rest of the organization won't buy in.

SHOTS 25—28

CHAPTER — 08

Q'S—BUILDING COMPETITIVE ADVANTAGE

We live in the Age of Now, an era of instant connections. People to cars to homes to toothbrushes, everything connects. Beam me up, Scotty! For business, it is the Wild West reloaded because you are either quick or dead. The thoroughfare is global, unforgiving and super-connected. The market is see-through, with no place to hide.

On this battlefield, survivors are leaders and leaders are fighters. NFL coach Vince Lombardi sets the play: "Running a football team is no different than running any other kind of organization—an army, a political party, or a business. The principles are the same. The object is to win—to beat the other guy. Maybe that sounds hard or cruel. I don't think it is."

Business is won and lost at frenetic pace. We live in an accelerated era of teens in T-shirts creating billion dollar companies overnight. We live in a disruptive era where industries can disappear in weeks. We live in a demanding era where people with ideas rule, not institutions. People have searching power, comparing power, sharing power, switching power, and destroying power.

Success in business used to require just your head. In the connected era, you need head, heart, tech, and speed, all to the power of an idea. The equation for winning is $(IQ + EQ + TQ + BQ)^{CQ}$.

To build a career, a company, or an empire in the Metaverse, you must run all four quotients. Get these four quotients humming—or be left in the dust.

Intellectual Quotient

Success starts with a smart view of the world, and it really is but a

SIX PRINCIPLES OF JUGAAD

Seek opportunity in adversity	1
Do more with less	2
Think and act flexibly	3
Keep it simple	4
Include the margin	5
Follow your heart	6

Jugaad Innovation: Think Frugal, Be Flexible, Generate Breakthrough Growth
by Navi Radjou, Jaideep Prabhu, Simone Ahuja.

start. Everyone in the hunt is smart because smarts are just a click, tap, or swipe away. An ocean of information is on tap. So be informed, be learning, be intelligent, and be stimulating your IQ daily. I may not be the smartest guy in any room, but bet your lunch I am the best prepared.

Generalists and specialists both matter. The world needs both. But it has never been easier to access technical expertise, never simpler to buy specialist brains. It is less easy to understand how things connect, to connect the dots, to create new dots, and to build lines into the future.

"Understanding is a path, not a point. It's a path of connections between thought and thought; patterns over patterns."

—TED founder Richard Saul Wurman

In the age of connectivity, the intersections are everything because they lead people to better places. A leader crosses the streams and creates priceless value off deep vaults of knowledge. As a working class kid I used to read the Latin classics in bed by torchlight. Build your knowledge platform early by being curious, reading widely, and networking madly. Few people are likely to have the breadth and depth of Leonardo da Vinci—an engineer, mathematician, architect, painter, sculptor, cartographer, botanist, and inventor—but knowing a lot of stuff about a lot of stuff is a good starting point.

Expand your frame of reference all you can. Disappear in book stores, rummage around the Internet, journey through history, scan engineering manuals, read the classics, bone up on conspiracy theories, explore physically and virtually. Howard Schultz's inspiration for Starbucks as a European-style coffeehouse came from a visit to Italy.

A top IQ searches for really good problems, because a good question is worth more than a good answer. Physicist Isador Isaac Rabi, who won the Nobel Prize, reportedly said: "My mother made me a scientist without ever intending it. Every other Jewish mother in Brooklyn would ask her child after school: 'So? Did you learn anything today?' But not my mother. She always asked me a different question. 'Izzy,' she would say, 'did you ask a good question today?' That difference—asking good questions—made me become a scientist!"

Every enterprise needs a unique intellectual point of view just to compete in a high-speed world. Leaders must lead. What is your unique point of view? What distances you from the pack? I asked business: what lies beyond brands? Saatchi & Saatchi got speed with the simplicity of Lovemarks—no brand manual required. Brands are about the people who make them. Lovemarks are about the people who love them. Lovemarks go straight for the heart.

Intellectual intelligence is base camp for an ascent to Peak Performance. Companies that hire dummies die. The IQ in the competitive advantage equation demands that companies hire the smartest people for the role. Most of us emit shades of both brilliance and dimness. It just depends on the task. Hire me in any role that needs a leader. Fire me in a trade that demands a unique craft. I can't write an ad, but I can recognize a great selling idea amidst merely good ones.

"Practical intelligence" is also part of IQ because fast times demand short cuts. Leaders need to improvise in a crazy world. Leaders learn to "MacGyver" and make do. They master the innovative Indian frugal work-around known as Jugaad. Leaders adapt, improvise, and catalyze.

Ernest Rutherford, the man who split the atom and who had a penchant for creating innovative experiments to solve problems, said of the lean, scrappy, and pragmatic research environment of New Zealand in the 1890s: "We don't have the money, so we have to think."

Emotional Quotient

Many companies have high IQ but suffer from low EQ. It is high EQ that counts now. Emotion fuels the twin driving forces of today. Not strategy and efficiency, but connectivity and creativity.

Reengineering, restructuring, and "re-everything" in business have exhausted people, and they haven't got us to a brighter, shinier future anyway. The connected world runs on the power of an idea, and all great ideas are fueled by one thing—passionate emotion.

The more ideas you have, the more you will succeed. Giant leaps come from intuition, instinct, and imagination, not from computations. Big data is the launch pad, but big emotion is how people create new worlds.

It is a leader's capacity to dream, to feel the rhythm of a problem, to gain empathetic insight into the issue, and then empower the team to hurtle towards greatness. Or as former attack and head coach of the England rugby union team Brian Ashton describes the "secrets" of the All Blacks:
- Win the ball.
- Win the space in front of them (i.e., go forward).
- Win the battle for continuity.
- Win the fight to set the tempo.
- Score tries.

At the ground level of business, creative foresight is about understanding how customers *feel*. Data tells us what people say and do, not how they feel. Great products and experiences are based on being empathetic and intuitive, not on being a calculator. Most insights are not insightful. They are repackaged information. You want a hard truth

THE MBA REFRAMED: MAKER OF BRILLIANT ADVANCEMENTS

Learn how to bring joy to your workplace. [1]

Learn a new sport or attend a physical boot camp. [2]

Read the top 20 books you've never read
(starting with *Don Quixote* and *Catch-22*). [3]

Become an alchemist—combining creativity and technology. [4]

Complete an art appreciation program. [5]

Invest in negotiation skills, including a study of the best
songwriters and their phrasing/persuasive skills. [6]

Become a brilliant salesman or woman. [7]

Develop a startup with a storytelling element. [8]

Make at least 500 Facebook friends before graduating. [9]

Learn a bit of business strategy (or just immerse yourself
in Drucker). [10]

that glows. Give me the hairy anthropologists over the research vampires and digital ninjas any day. You've got to interpret it. You have to feel it.

Because we have a dilemma, a shocker, and we must fix it quick. Companies worldwide rely on MBA-schooled managers to interpret the world and to unleash creativity.

Many management schools today have not caught up with the VUCA world we live in, or the key trigger points of their Millennial students. The MBA needs a reframe. MBA = Master of Business Administration. "Master" means you stop learning. "Business" misfires on creativity. And what do business schools churn out—administrators! Edward de Bono told me: "There's no use being brilliant at the wrong thing."

Business schools focus on rationality, equations, analysis, and data. A good foundation. But then what? They overload IQ and they bench EQ. They teach strategy but do not provide enough learning on execution; they teach process instead of sentience—the ability to feel, perceive, or experience subjectively.

"The consumer isn't a moron; she is your wife."

— David Ogilvy

SHOTS 29—32

Many freshly minted MBAs exit management school with no personal purpose, poor negotiation skills, and a low emotional quotient. Down the track you get a train wreck. Today's MBAs can look like doctors parachuting into a foreign-language country with no bedside manner.

There's a lot in common with general high school. Much of the teaching at schools is a waste of time. It is forgotten and even resented the day you leave school. Albert Einstein: "Education is what remains after one has forgotten what one has learned in school."

Every MBA student I encounter is exhausted. Tell me why that is good? Schools throw course work at students. It's like *The Hunger Games* or SEAL training: survival of the fittest. Business needs the greatest. The most inspirational. The quickest. Not just marathoners.

Business schools can narrow people down instead of equipping them for the broad world of business.

I did my MBA at Procter & Gamble. I'm an uneducated professor. I was kicked out of school for the wrong reasons. Now I teach MBAs in order to subvert the education system. I teach them how to win through dexterity, velocity, and integrity. Bruce Wayne gets to be Batman. Students and teachers love the flailing of orthodoxy.

To get to the future first, check that your EQ is well developed, and don't join an organization with low EQ. Emotional intelligence is by far the most important dimension in an enterprising life. The ability to make emotional connections with colleagues, partners, clients, stakeholders, consumers—any audience—is the defining skill of your future.

Technological Quotient

What a world we live in. It's a world where machines talk back to people, vehicles drive themselves, house lights turn themselves off, mail and medicine come from the sky, energy is generated from the sun and the wind, storage is in a cloud, footprints are digital, and trolls have computers.

The pace of technology is blistering, disrupting, and exciting. The immense promise of technology is transforming everything from transport, energy, and agriculture to healthcare, education, and retailing. I have no fears about technology and believe it offers more opportunity for prosperity and harmony than any other phenomenon in history. As for any problems, we will work them out. It's a 90/10 equation between opportunities and issues.

Technology is embedded in modern living, and you need TQ just to compete in life. I'm either the worst or the best person to talk about technology. Apart from my core iPhone utilities and apps, my most sophisticated use of tech is my trusty Montblanc pen, mighty and deadly as it is!

Technology has to be basic. It has to be easy for anyone to use. TQ means technical eloquence, empathetic design, and intuitive use. Nowadays there is a user at the end of every business line with a short fuse and a long reach.

Treat technology as a critical enabler, not the differentiator. The trick is to make this magic wand your slave, and not to become its slave. Most companies and most executives are unwittingly vanquished by technology, especially if born pre-Internet. Most organizations and people are faking it to their hearts' content. They don't use tech for their benefit. A company needs a broad vision and incremental approach to technology. Bite off too much, it will bruise the CFO.

Having TQ is not about being a nerd or a technophile. It is about knowing what tech is out there, staying on top of it, and bending it to your will in business and in life.

Have you been enslaved? A leader can't be. A leader takes charge. A leader resists the machine. I have conversations with strangers in elevators rather than bury my head in a device to check the latest incoming. I feel completely in charge of my own technology. I can enjoy solitude and contemplation and yet feel open to the world. Most CEOs live in a bunker. I'm open to the world and most correspondents get a hand-written reply within 24 hours. I was known in PepsiCo as the person who gave instantaneous responses.

A golden rule is no screens at the dinner table or in the bedroom. iPhone-interruptus is a blight on conversation and dreams. Parents take the path of least resistance and allow their children unfettered screen time. It's one of the few areas in which I counsel moderation in favor of excess.

Bloody Quick!

Relentless execution is the killer app. I learned this working at Procter & Gamble 35 years ago. Today it's crucial. In a high-speed world, be bloody quick or be beaten bloody.

You can't be consensus-driven, process-driven, or horizon-driven today. You have to be now-driven. The pace of change, the speed of culture, and the immediacy of demand requires this. If you are not bloody quick, your competition will eat your breakfast, lunch, and dinner.

A business leader takes the enterprise from strategic to ballistic, whether the business is curing diseases, transiting people, delivering daily sustenance, communicating ideas, or exploring space.

Velocity defeats strategy. In 2012, at an Institute of Directors conference at the 02 Arena in London, I proffered to senior business leaders that strategy is dead. It created a ruckus. Chess Grand Master Savielly Tartakower was driving this truck ages ago: "Tactics is what you do when there is something to do; strategy is what you do when there is nothing to do."

Classically, a leader does three things: assess, decide, and execute. Leaders spend half their time interrogating the data, checking the facts and assessing. They spend 30 percent on discussion and consensus. The other 20 percent—execution—is a hospital pass to some poor sucker down the line. This is most businesses today: strategically driven, by-the-book, MBA-obsessed, ponderous.

In a crazy world, this model fails. Today, spend just 20 percent of your time assessing, because there is nothing to interrogate. Everyone has the same information, mountains of it. The information has surrendered. It's waving a white flag, saying, "Here I am, take me!" More than ever, a leader must decide, not dither. Decide from the gut; decide now. Use your emotional quotient, because it's amazing shorthand. Spend only 10 percent of your time on decision-making. Then spend the remaining 70 percent executing and driving it home remorselessly.

In turbulent times, a leader is navigating, surfing, flexing, and course-correcting every day. The leader is close to the audience, feeling its pulse, testing ideas, tasting success, and applying the mantra of former Coca-Cola boss Roberto Goizueta: Meet, Beat, Repeat.

Focus on what counts. A 100-day plan is bloody quick. It's about action. It takes commitment. List 10 things to achieve over the next 100 days. Start each plan with an action verb. Make them stretchy, real, and measurable actions. Hit double digits. Get the account. Design the app. Cure the disease. Win the campaign. End the war.

Cross off at least half the items on your list. Decide what goes and what stays based on importance, not urgency. Get started. In 100 days, go again. Make your life an endless journey of 100 days plans. You'll smoke everyone around you.

IQ+EQ+TQ+BQ are then all raised to the CQ quotient. What's CQ? That's the special sauce, the X-factor, the brand promise, the irresistible component that provides exponential power. It's an element that varies from business to business. At Saatchi & Saatchi, that C stands for "creativity." For a retailer, that C stands for "customers" (how to be faster, more convenient). If you're a professional services firm, C is the "client." At The Ritz-Carlton, legendary for the incredible investments it makes in employee training and development, C stands for "colleagues." The key is to identify your C quotient—then amplify it!

SHOTS 29—32

THE 64 SHOTS

Andy Warhol

ARTIST

Bob Dylan

POET

John F. Kennedy

35TH PRESIDENT OF THE UNITED STATES

Dr. Martin Luther King, Jr.

CIVIL RIGHTS LEADER

Muhammad Ali

WORLD HEAVYWEIGHT BOXING CHAMPION

Nelson Mandela

PRESIDENT, SOUTH AFRICA

Winston Churchill

PRIME MINISTER, UNITED KINGDOM

Margaret Thatcher

PRIME MINISTER, UNITED KINGDOM

Ernest Rutherford

PHYSICIST, NOBEL LAUREATE

Albert Einstein

PHYSICIST, NOBEL LAUREATE

Shimon Peres

PRESIDENT, ISRAEL

Leonard Cohen

POET

Clarence Clemons

SAXOPHONIST

Bruce Springsteen

SONGWRITER

Mary Quant

DESIGNER

Vivienne Westwood

DESIGNER

Twiggy

MODEL

Brigitte Bardot

ACTRESS

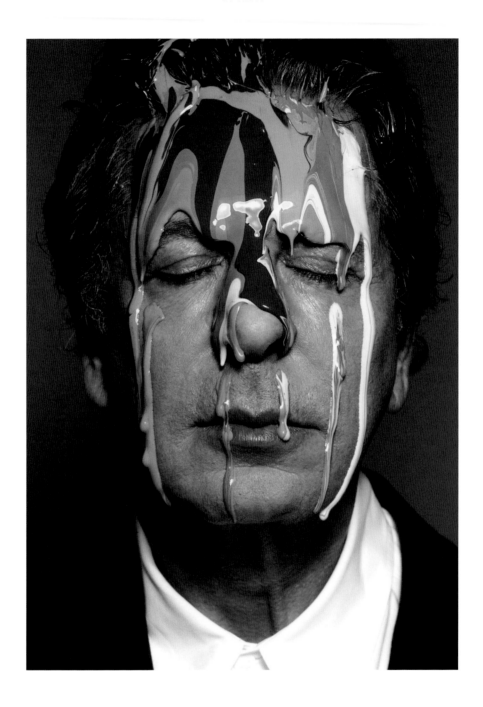

Charles Saatchi

CO-FOUNDER, SAATCHI & SAATCHI

Maurice Saatchi

CO-FOUNDER, SAATCHI & SAATCHI

Bob Seelert

CHAIRMAN EMERITUS, SAATCHI & SAATCHI

Maurice Lévy

CEO, PUBLICIS GROUPE

Daniel Dennett

PHILOSOPHER

Rowan Williams

THEOLOGIAN

George Bernard Shaw

PLAYWRIGHT, NOBEL LAUREATE

Lee Child

AUTHOR, JACK REACHER NOVELS

Norman Schwarzkopf

FOUR-STAR GENERAL

Colin Powell

FOUR-STAR GENERAL

Russell Crowe

ACTOR

Renzo Rosso

FOUNDER, DIESEL

Peter Drucker

MANAGEMENT THEORIST

Wanda Ferragamo

BUSINESS MATRIARCH

A.G. Lafley

PROCTER & GAMBLE LEADER

Akio Toyoda

CEO, TOYOTA

Steve Jobs

CO-FOUNDER, APPLE

Jeff Bezos

FOUNDER, AMAZON

Tom Peters

BUSINESS MAVERICK

Alan Webber

CO-FOUNDER, *FAST COMPANY*

Mihaly Csikszentmihalyi

ARCHITECT OF FLOW

Don Miguel Ruiz

AUTHOR, *THE FOUR AGREEMENTS*

Roger Enrico

PEPSICO MAVERICK

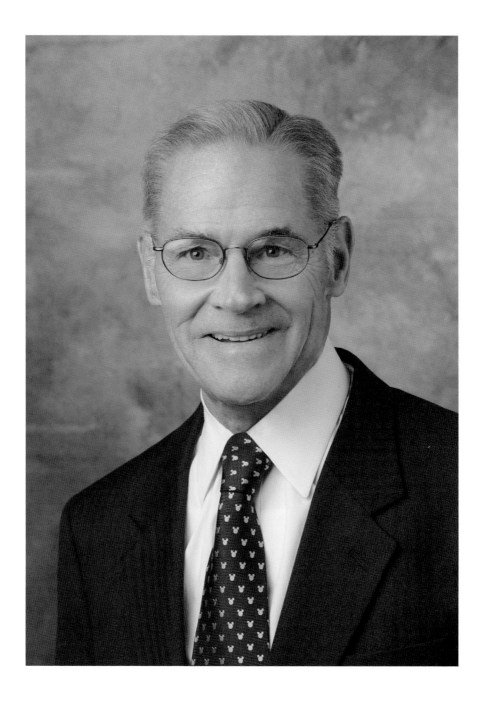

John Pepper

PROCTER & GAMBLE LEADER

Herve Humler

CEO, THE RITZ-CARLTON

Edward de Bono

Theresa Gattung

NEW ZEALAND BUSINESS LEADER

Yoshio Ishizaka

TOYOTA LEADER

John Key

NEW ZEALAND PRIME MINISTER

John Kirwan

ALL BLACK

Mike Summerbee

MANCHESTER CITY FOOTBALLER

Colin Bell

MANCHESTER CITY FOOTBALLER

Edmund Hillary

EVEREST MOUNTAINEER

Rewi Alley

FOUNDER, CHINESE WORK COOPERATIVE MOVEMENT

Vince Lombardi

NFL COACH

Peter Blake

SAILOR

Sean Fitzpatrick

ALL BLACKS CAPTAIN

Richie McCaw

ALL BLACKS CAPTAIN

Brian Ashton

ENGLAND RUGBY COACH

Brian Lochore

ALL BLACK

Chris Laidlaw

ALL BLACK

Earle Kirton

ALL BLACK

Gilbert Enoka

ALL BLACKS MENTAL SKILLS COACH

Jonah Lomu

ALL BLACK

William Shatner & Leonard Nimoy

KIRK & SPOCK

Clayton Moore

THE LONE RANGER

Andy Warhol
Bob Dylan
John F. Kennedy
Martin Luther King, Jr.
Muhammad Ali
Nelson Mandela
Winston Churchill
Margaret Thatcher
Ernest Rutherford
Albert Einstein
Shimon Peres
Leonard Cohen
Clarence Clemons
Bruce Springsteen
Mary Quant
Vivienne Westwood
Twiggy
Brigitte Bardot
Charles Saatchi
Maurice Saatchi
Bob Seelert
Maurice Lévy
Daniel Dennett
Rowan Williams
George Bernard Shaw
Lee Child
Norman Schwarzkopf
Colin Powell
Russell Crowe
Renzo Rosso
Peter Drucker
Wanda Ferragamo

A.G. Lafley
Akio Toyoda
Steve Jobs
Jeff Bezos
Tom Peters
Alan Webber
Mihaly Csikszenthmihalyi
Don Miguel Ruiz
Roger Enrico
John Pepper
Herve Hummler
Edward de Bono
Theresa Gattung
Yoshio Ishizaka
John Key
John Kirwan
Mike Summerbee
Colin Bell
Edmund Hillary
Rewi Alley
Vince Lombardi
Peter Blake
Sean Fitzpatrick
Richie McCaw
Brian Ashton
Brian Lochore
Chris Laidlaw
Earle Kirton
Gilbert Enoka
Jonah Lomu
Kirk & Spock
The Lone Ranger

"Look, don't see, listen, don't hear.
The more you engage, the longer you survive."

— Jack Reacher

CHAPTER — 09

INSTILLING THE I WORDS

INSPIRATION
N
T
U
IDEAS
T
IMPACT
O
N

Inspiration

I grew up in Lancaster in the northwest of England. My mother worked in a shop and my father worked in a mental hospital as a security guard. When I was 14, Peter Sampson, an inspirational English teacher, had us share our dreams. I wanted to be a millionaire by 30. Everyone laughed, but I was serious. It seemed to me—to quote the Wizard of Id's golden rule: "He who has the gold makes the rules."

My mother was a pessimist. My sister Trisha and I decided to rebel against that, to create our own worlds. We both believed we could live the big life and change things for the better.

Our dream came to life through the I's and E's. Leaders with the I's and E's make it. They can do anything, and the first of the I words drives everything. Inspiration is a turbocharger. Careers, companies, causes, and countries rise up on inspiration. The crazier things get, the harder this I word works.

A leader is inspired to deliver. A leader inspires others to deliver in pursuit of a dream. The leader gives people responsibility, learning, recognition, and joy to bring the dream to life. These four emotional thrusters will accelerate any team to reach any summit.

Inspiration means *to breathe spirit into*. Spirit is the animating energy within living things. Spirit is liveliness, vivacity, and vigor of mind. It is the emotion that determines your character. It is the readiness to assert oneself and to be counted.

An inspirational leader stands for an idea, pours belief into people, and makes them feel loved. Inspirers are the crazies, the empathizers, the engagers, the "go to" people—because they make things happen.

Inspirers are giants whose shoulders you stand on. Herbert Schmitz at Procter & Gamble was the most inspirational person I've ever worked with. Selling volume is strategic, according to Herbert. Execution rules. At PepsiCo, there was a guy named Bob Beeby. He was head of international. He took care of me, supported, and protected me. At the same time, he pushed me forward. When I was overthinking a problem, second-guessing myself, he sent me a picture of a bridge that seemed to go on into infinity. The caption read: "We'll cross that bridge when we come to it."

Leaders are teachers. A friend, John Wareham, is a leadership psychologist, lecturer, and writer. He overcame a stutter and not only became a leading CEO recruiter and coach, he also created a life-changing communication program for inmates at New York's Rikers Island prison, the world's largest penal colony. Inspiration is a guy with a speech impediment becoming an orator and teaching philosophy and poetry to a group of felons wanting to break the cycle of their lives.

Leaders inspire everyone they touch. To run for office, to design a store, to win a trophy, to raise a family, to change a destiny, the first thing to pour in is inspiration. People like to be informed, people want to be involved, but people love to be inspired.

Ideas

It took the telephone 75 years to reach 50 million users. It took the Angry Birds app 35 days.

The world is connected and connecting, but connectivity is not the currency. At the heart of all these connections is the ultimate driving force, the idea. Ideas are reframing every industry there is. Technology enables them, but it is the idea that is the currency of today.

Ideas have unreasonable power. Ideas—not strategy, efficiency, or effectiveness—have magical power. We are living in the Age of the Idea. And the cultures with the most original ideas are best placed to win. Ideas have soft power. Shimon Peres:

"It is a new world. You may have the strongest army— but it cannot conquer ideas, it cannot conquer knowledge."

SHOTS 33—36

Building a business from an idea is the hardest and most satisfying and rewarding thing you can do in life. What is creativity in business? Figuring out if there is a gap in the market, and then if there is a market in the gap. Creativity in business usually solves a problem, sometimes before we know it exists. Almost everything in business can present itself as a problem to be solved. Creativity surfaces when someone defines in one line a clear business problem. Lift-off demands an idea. In communications, "content" is just noise without an idea at the center.

Creative magic is an idea that gets to future first. The power of an idea is intense, from Gutenberg's movable type printing and Marie Curie's radioactive breakthroughs, through to speedster-creators like Google and Amazon.

How do you spark a great idea? Connect stuff. Creativity isn't some mysterious outcome of deep contemplation. It is a noisy, involving, fast-moving dynamic that draws from art, culture, sport, media, entertainment, history, politics, and commerce. It is a collision sport where people interact, knowledge spills over, and thoughts career off in new directions.

When planning Pixar's headquarters, Steve Jobs made it impossible for people not to run into each other. Rub some smart people with different opinions together and see what happens.

To be creative, reframe, reframe, reframe. When Bob Dylan went from acoustic to electric at the Newport Folk Festival, he changed music and politics at the same time. A Saatchi & Saatchi challenge was to reposition the image of a war-torn violent country into a place of future hope and brightness. The nation of Kosovo was framed as the "Young Europeans."

Creativity is also about removing complexity. Colin Powell: "Great leaders are almost always great simplifiers, who can cut through argument, debate, and doubt, to offer a solution everybody can understand." Thomas Jefferson began a letter to a fellow Founding Father by apologizing: "If I had more time, this letter would be shorter."

The Holy Grail is a big idea. You need to ask the right question, because big ideas are simply questions in search of an answer. Be open to inspiration at all times of the day. Archimedes had his eureka moment in the bath tub. And be persistent. Edison was awarded 1,093 patents.

You'll be lucky to have one big idea in your lifetime. If you do, go for it for all you are worth. You'll know it when lightning strikes. Einstein as he cracked the special theory of relativity: "a storm broke loose in my mind."

Intuition

You are a leader who has inspired people to be the best they can be in pursuit of a dream. Their hearts are pumping. Their heads are fizzing. Their feet are twitching. They have the strands of an idea. What enables them to produce a humdinger?

Is it because they have instinct? Instinct is a start. Instinct is indispensable. You want to be born with instinct. In crazy times demanding instant action, you're screwed without it.

But just surviving is no fun. To get from surviving to winning takes something more refined than instinct. It takes intuition. Instinct can't be trained. Intuition—a source of knowledge that calls upon attentiveness, empathy, and sensitivity—is a skill that can be trained and developed.

Intuition now has serious help from algorithms. Every industry, institution, and individual is impacted by big data. Data is enhancing every field, from traditional marketing, personalized healthcare, and crime prevention to risk management, fertility tracking, and energy provision.

Can you data mine, excavate, model, measure, predict, automate, track, monitor, and target your way to glory? Or do you go with your gut? A leader does both. On the one hand, wild swings lose games. On the other, the machine limits the dream. Worshiping logic ends a leader's trek to the stars. There's the Spock approach: "Captain, we are checkmated." There's the leader's gut: Captain Kirk: "Not Chess Mr. Spock—poker. Do you know the game?"

Intuition is an unproved feeling of truth. Nobel laureate Leon Lederman: "The essence of physics is pure faith. To believe something while knowing it cannot be proved (yet) is the essence of physics." A leader goes where no one has gone before. When you get to the fork in the road, don't lose faith in your hunch. Italian-American film director Frank Capra: "A hunch is creativity trying to tell you something."

Intuition is at the heads of many great rivers. Albert Einstein said that if he hadn't been a physicist he would have been a musician, because he felt his thinking was more rooted in intuition and imagery than logic and equations. Intuition made James Brown play every instrument like percussion. Intuition is what made Andy Warhol see the beauty in a soup can. It is David Beckham scorching a career-defining goal from halfway on the football field. It's why the All Blacks play rugby.

Intuition tells us who and what to love, which doesn't stand to reason. The things that change people's world usually don't. Trust in the sixth sense. It can see the future.

Impact

Without the last I word, it's all for nothing. Ideas are like rear ends, everyone has one. If an idea doesn't have impact it means nothing. It has been a useless exercise.

An idea is only an idea when it is executed and touches someone. I meet a lot of smart people who have plenty of ideas. Some are good. Most of them go nowhere. They go into a research paper, a focus group, a training run, but they never shift reality.

To lead in a crazy world, you need to create impact. Impact players don't just get things done. They make things happen. While others are talking, impact players are activating. They cause revelation, acceleration, inspiration, elevation, and jubilation.

Leaders are impact players. They are the best players in their position. In the intensity of elite rugby, a fly-half separates anarchy from harmony. The No.10, the equivalent of the quarterback, my position through my playing days, runs the game, makes the calls. The best in the fly-half position are magicians. For New Zealand, since 1987, that would be Grant Fox, Andrew Mehrtens, and Daniel Carter, impact players through and through. Rugby World Cups are won by impact players because the defenses are so tight and the contests are so even.

I spot the impact players in the MBA programs that I teach. The impact comes from their being and bearing. You see it flow through bright eyes, interesting postures, and lateral questions.

Impact players can take on mana, a word in the Maori language. Mana is a supernatural force. It can be earned by a person through his or her life. It is about prestige, bearing, authority, status, influence, spiritual power, control, and character. It includes charisma, but has far more depth.

Mana is not something you do or say. You don't need to perform. You simply are. A person with mana has huge presence. When a person with mana walks into a room, all goes quiet. Mana isn't claimed. People bestow it on you. Oftentimes you're the last to know you have it. Those with mana are impact players. Their very nature makes waves for others to surf on.

Be an impact player in your field. Light jabbers are just as good as big hitters. The greatest combatants often aren't the fiercest sluggers. Muhammad Ali would "float like a butterfly, sting like a bee." Ali outfoxed much heavier hitters like Frazier and Foreman. You can jab 64 times or go for the knockout punch. The key is for ideas to make impact.

A win is a win is a win.

CHAPTER — 10

EMBEDDING THE E WORDS

ENTHUSIASM
N
EMOTION
R
EDGE
Y

E words are my "go to" words. I use E words to drive conversations, frame presentations, and ignite organizations. Leaders win with the E's. For starters, a leader enables, empowers, engages, empathizes, excites, eliminates, and executes.

Four E words are embedded in leadership: enthusiasm, energy, emotion, and edge. They are indispensable for leadership: With these four E words, a leader can conquer his or her Everest.

Enthusiasm

Enthusiasm is out of this world. "Enthusiasm" is from the Greek, "enthousiasmos," which literally means "having the god within you." An enthusiast is an irresistible force of nature.

Entrepreneurs are enthusiasts. Mad Men are enthusiasts. Pirates are enthusiasts. Children are enthusiasts. My grandchildren are enthusiasts. They won't take no for an answer.

Enthusiasm is not just irresistible, it is unstoppable. French-Swiss writer Anne Louise Germaine de Staël was an intellectual, conversationalist, political activist, defender of women's rights, and collector of lovers. She lived in exile much of her life. Napoleon banished her from Paris. Madame de Staël said an irresistible thing: "Enthusiasm is the emotion that offers us the greatest happiness, the only one that offers it to us, the only one able to sustain human destiny in whatever situation destiny places us."

Enthusiasm is fundamental to organizations in a chaotic world. An enthusiast revels in adversity, and attacks the status quo. Companies don't just need change managers today. We are beyond that in these crazy times. Organizations need people who enjoy chaos. In turbulence, hire people who love chaos, revel in mayhem, and fly at the storm.

Vince Lombardi underlined the importance of enthusiasm: "If you aren't fired with enthusiasm, you will be fired with enthusiasm." I get approached every day with requests, such as speechmaking, endorsements, and employing people. The first thing I look for in a hire is enthusiasm.

"Success is the ability to go from one failure to another with no loss of enthusiasm."

— Winston Churchill

Leaders need enthusiasm because it is inspirational, motivational, and infectious. I've given 1,000+ speeches. I have been called many things after them. "Unenthusiastic" isn't one of them. Ninety-nine percent of presentations, pitches, and conversations in business are boring as bat scat. For any clutch presentation, make sure that your body and vocal language burst with enthusiasm. Exercise before a big meeting. If you don't exude energy, no one will believe it. Up, up, and away.

Emotion

Emotion is the decisive "E" because people run on emotion. People live with emotion, work with emotion, play with emotion, shop with emotion, and decide based on emotion. Emotion leads to action, and leadership is all about inspiring people to act.

Dale Carnegie, legendary corporate trainer and author of *How to Win Friends and Influence People* said: "When dealing with people, remember you are not dealing with creatures of logic, but creatures of emotion." Don't just remember it, know it.

The heart rules the head at decision time, from an executive facing a major decision through to a consumer standing in the snack aisle. Car guys ask each other, "How much metal did you move?" At Toyota, we changed the question to *"How much does the metal move you?"* If you are selling a big ticket item, you want to be resonating with emotion.

People spend most of their days at work. You can't expect to keep emotion out of the workplace when the workplace is filled with emotional creatures. Why would you? The trick is to learn to harness the power of emotion—*all* the colors of the emotional palette—and create success. This applies whether you are facing colleagues, consumers, or customers. To me, B2B (business-to-business) is just P2P (person-to-person). It's more personal than B2C (business-to-consumer).

Leaders master emotion; emotion doesn't master leaders. "Success in investing doesn't correlate with IQ once you're about the level of 25," said Warren Buffett, the Oracle of Omaha. "Once you have ordinary intelligence, what you need is the temperament to control the urges that get other people into trouble investing." Emotional intelligence is a two-way mirror. It's as much about self-assessment, self-regulation, and self-monitoring—having a strong Spidey sense about how others respond to you—as it is about reading the emotional temperature of a room or understanding the motives of others.

SHOTS 37—40

When reason is applied to emotion, it comes up with more negatives than positives. There have been many attempts at charting the emotional map. Aristotle, as early as 4 B.C., deduced 14 irreducible emotions, which he described as fear, confidence, anger, friendship, calm, enmity, shame, shamelessness, pity, kindness, envy, indignation, emulation, and contempt. Darwin had a go in his book *The Expression of the Emotions in Man and Animals.* Mostly recently, researchers at the University of Glasgow, following a detailed study of facial expressions, reduced the basic emotions to four: anger, fear, happiness, and sadness.

Me? I'm with the songwriter Johnny Mercer: "Accentuate the positive, eliminate the negative." When asked whether he was worried during the 2015 Rugby World Cup final between New Zealand and Australia played at Twickenham, England, to a televised audience of 120 million people, when Australia surged back to within four points, All Blacks coach Steve Hansen laconically replied: "Worry is such a wasted emotion." History will record that the greatest team in world sport went on to win by a 17-point margin, 34-17.

It is remarkable how emotional meaning gets made. In a famous study, Albert Mehrabian, Professor Emeritus of Psychology at UCLA, uncovered the "7%-38%-55%" rule. What Professor Mehrabian found was that in face-to-face interactions, only 7 percent of emotional meaning comes from the words the speaker used, 38 percent from tone of voice, and 55 percent from body language. Leaders understand this truth—it's not what you say, it's how you say it!

Great leaders are master storytellers, inspired communicators, and conductors of emotion. In a *New Yorker* essay titled "One Year: Storyteller-in-Chief," Pulitzer Prize-winning novelist Junot Diaz wrote: "...one of a President's primary responsibilities is to be a storyteller... If a President is to have any success, if his policies are going to gain any kind of traction among the electorate, he first has to tell us a story." Great leaders know how to access emotions, how to direct them, how to amplify them.

Having worked for a brewer, I know beer. Each American political cycle the press, pundits, and pontificators ask: "With which candidate would you most want to have a beer?" What are they really asking? It's not who is most qualified, intelligent, worthy, or even, I'd argue, likable. It's who is the most relatable, authentic, and emotionally accessible. U.S. Presidents are—apart from everything else—America's biggest TV star, entering into homes every night. In the modern TV era—with the notable exception of Nixon, whose emotional spectrum fluctuated between self-loathing and paranoia—it is always the more personable candidate who wins.

David Axelrod, President Obama's chief campaign strategist—reflecting on Hillary Clinton's failed 2008 presidential bid—spoke about what was perceived to be her authenticity problem. "Voters don't like to be told that their decision is predetermined," Axelrod said. *"They want to be asked for their vote and more than that they want to have a genuine connection with the candidate."* It's not an accident that the high point of Clinton's first presidential run was when she got choked up at a New Hampshire diner, "found her voice," and went on to win a surprise victory in that key primary state the next day.

Chewed down to the bone, leadership is emotional mastery. Whether extroverted or introverted, it is the power of an emotional connection. Great leaders are master psychologists, team coaches, cheerleaders, referees, hostage negotiators, Spielberg-level storytellers, mom and dad, and your favorite schoolteacher. Being students of emotion allows them to be all those things, to play all those roles, and to do it authentically. Let emotion rip!

Energy

A leader is called on to have energy. Energy is power. Energy is zest, vigor, exuberance, and dynamism. Energy is the color of passion, optimism, and love. Energy activates, ignites, and transforms.

WINNING BEHAVIOR

LOSING PLAYERS	WINNING PLAYERS
Independent	**Interdependent**
Me, my, I	**We, our, us**
Point the finger	**Shine the spotlight**
Fearlead	**Cheerlead**
Waste time	**Value time**
Pass the buck	**Pass the ball**
Cause stress	**Spread calm**
Procrastinate	**Instigate**
Castigate	**Collaborate**
Instruct	**Inspire**
Sap energy	**Zap energy**
Create uncertainty	**Foster fun**
We're done	**We're not done yet**

A leader should radiate energy for people to plug into, to rev up on, and to go to work with.

"Leaders are like the wind. You don't see the wind but you can see all around you what the effect of it is," said George Kohlrieser, leadership expert, psychologist, and veteran hostage negotiator.

The leader turns negative energy into positive energy. Positivity generates the winning behaviors in any organization. Creativity is the leader's priority, and ideas require the spark of energy. They require vitality, vim, and oomph.

There are different ways to spark energy. Theater is helpful because it creates momentum and can tip the scales. When I was CEO of Pepsi-Cola Canada in the late 1980s, we had been second to Coke for an eon. I reckoned if we could take our guys over the edge, we could get leadership. We did.

To celebrate what felt like a once-in-a-lifetime milestone, I organized a presentation in Toronto for our bottlers, retail partners, media, and civic leaders. The context of the event was free trade. The Prime Minister of Canada, Brian Mulroney, was there. I endorsed the idea of competition, and its benefits for Canada. I talked about how Pepsi in Canada was a company driven by local entrepreneurs, versus Coke being owned by the U.S. company. Then the theater curtains opened. Out trundled a big Coca-Cola vending machine. I put on safety goggles, picked up a machine gun, and blew it to pieces.

Everyone hit the floor, ducked for cover. The noise was shattering, the damage even more so. But it was theatrics all the way, a totally safe operation. I had enlisted the co-operation of the Canadian Mounties to supervise, we used blanks, and the machine was rigged. The media went nuts. The line was: "Here's Pepsi—going past Coke." My sales guys fielded "that crazy guy" talking point on every call. It was an instant success. Shock and awe jolted the team over the edge. It is vital to turn up with zip, zap, and zig. Make a show of it.

SHOTS 37—40

Energy use must be focused, because leadership is pressured, times are fast, and big-city living is draining. Take time for family and friends; this is where true happiness comes from. Take time for fun and celebration. Take time for rest and quiet. Get away to the mountains, bush, desert, and beach. I have a sanctuary in Grasmere, a sleepy village in the Lake District in England. The poet William Wordsworth lived in Grasmere for 14 years and declared the Vale "the loveliest spot that man hath ever found."

I escape to the desert in Arizona; I love the Wild West. And to a bush haven in Auckland, New Zealand, truly out on the edge. Escape to wild places in order to center, reflect, regroup, and recharge your creative energies. Silence can break down the barriers to creativity. The sessions that I run for leaders are in faraway retreats.

Good energy gets you in the zone, juicing creativity. The zone demands physical, mental, and spiritual health. Exercise well, sleep well, eat well, feel well, and give well—and you will lead.

Edge

"The simple answer is usually the correct one," said Saul Berenson in *Homeland*. Enthusiasm, emotion, and energy lead to the Edge. This is where creativity comes from.

My partner-in-crime, Brian Sweeney, once had a car ride to Auckland's Wild West, Karekare, with Kevin Kelly, founding editor of *Wired,* who introduced him to Stephen Jay Gould's theory of punctuated equilibrium. The geographical magnet that drew me to New Zealand suddenly made sense. "Punk Eek" is the idea that change in a species happens first on the edge of the species, out on the margins, away from centers, in extremities where the population is most sparse and new forms of life are free to emerge.

Innovation struggles to come from the center because the middle is too crowded, orthodox, and muddled. Change is at the cutting, leading, bleeding edge. Edge zones today are dynamic, uninhibited, and not bound by history. "It can't be done" doesn't exist on the Edge. When I was headhunted to New Zealand in 1989 by Douglas Myers to operational-ize his Asia Pacific brewing vision, it was like being transplanted into a place that the upper class hadn't ruined. New Zealand is a classic Edge zone—remote, restless, unfiltered, egalitarian, and a place of unlikely firsts. New Zealanders split the atom (Rutherford), gave women the vote first (Sheppard), conquered Mt. Everest (Hillary), and were first to fly (Pearse).

My dream for New Zealand is to "win the world from the Edge." Don't get sucked into the center. The further you are from the center, the more ideas will come into view. "I want to stay as close to the edge as I can without going over. Out on the edge you see all kinds of things you can't see from the center," said *Slaughterhouse-Five* author Kurt Vonnegut. Edge is more the territory of novelists than management theorists, though the exception is proven with a critical 2003 book *The Deviant's Advantage: How Fringe Ideas Create Mass Markets* by Watts Wacker and Ryan Mathews.

Today's winning teams are dream chasers, risk takers, and rule breakers. Cecil Beaton, English photographer: "Be daring, be differ-ent, be impractical, be anything that will assert integrity of purpose and imaginative vision against the play-it-safers, the creatures of the commonplace, the slaves of the ordinary." My early career breaks came from being impractical. I went to Mary Quant in London. I said: "I'm 19, I speak French and Spanish, and I work really hard. I'm three times smarter than anyone else you've got, and whatever you are paying them, I'll work for half."

The Edge is where creativity cuts loose in the Age of Idea. Leaders go to the Edge.

SHOTS 37—40

CHAPTER — 11

WHAT CREATIVE LEADERS DO

The plodding era of strategy is being retired by a scorching era of creativity. To create a culture where ideas rule, you must become a Creative Leader. There is a premium on originality. Building creative environments, inspiring creative ideas, finding creative solutions—these are the signatures of peak performing organizations. I call this the SuperVUCA challenge, the drive to create outcomes that are V-ibrant, U-nreal, C-razy, and A-stounding. In a SuperVUCA world, the crazies reign and the speed demons rule. There are four primary things Creative Leaders do.

Change the Language

In making Winston Churchill an honorary citizen of the United States, President John F. Kennedy said: "He mobilized the English language and sent it into battle."

Revolution begins with language. Change the language and you can change everything.

If you want people to join you, work for you, partner with you, buy from you, talk about you, speed your cause, then you need language that inspires people.

Most companies use the wrong language. Spanish Emperor Charles V reportedly said: "I speak Spanish to God, Italian to women, French to men, and German to my horse." Most companies mix this up.

Creative Leaders invent their own language. They create a system of meaning understood by everyone that binds people together, founded on the values of the group. They invent a unique vocabulary, shorthand for communicating cultural norms and standards. The Creative Leader tells stories around the campfire of shared values.

Apple is a strong example: Think Different; Stay hungry. Stay foolish; Why join the Navy when you can be a pirate? Popular potent examples range from Once a Marine Always a Marine, to Inspire a Generation, to I Love New York, to I Have a Dream.

Dr. Martin Luther King, Jr., like President Lincoln before him, positioned civil rights as a struggle for the moral soul of the nation rather than as about the inclusion of any one particular group. He once said:

"I have decided to stick with love. Hate is too great a burden to bear."

Advocating for the right to transportation, equal hiring, education, and political engagement was standard during the civil rights era. It was smarter to champion the rights of all against inequality and those who enforced it.

The right language can create higher orders of relationship, business, product, service, design, and performance. *Fast Company* co-founder Alan Webber reminded me that it can create entire new categories. A premise of Lovemarks is that you change the world with one word.

Change the language and you can change anything. I don't believe we will make the planet a better place with the word "sustainable." That's bland brand language. It is about maintaining when it should be about transforming. It is about anxiety when it should be about opportunity. Dr. King did not say "I have a nightmare." He said: "I have a dream."

We need a dream. We need to inspire a worldwide movement of personal activations that is irresistible.

Have Lots of Ideas

A growth company is an ideas company, an ideas company has an ideas culture, and an ideas culture means leaders running lots of ideas continuously. The winner of today is not the company bent on one big idea. It is the company with the most ideas. It is the company with a non-stop production line of small ideas day after day.

Double Nobel Prize winner Dr. Linus Pauling said the way to get a good idea is to have lots of ideas. A Creative Leader has a plethora of ideas. In this Age of Now, you have to be relentless about having ideas.

I get asked all the time what the future holds. I don't have a clue. Neither does anyone who says they do. You can't see the future, so hack your way in. The hacker recognizes that big ideas are scarce, strung out over time, and investment-hungry. Get to your big idea by having lots of small ideas and testing them quickly, cheaply, and widely. Chances are your customer or your audience will turn one of your 20 small ideas into a big one.

Chances are someone will try to stop you too. Ideas are fragile and most organizations murder them at birth. Keep yours moving, adjust them on the fly, and don't let the "Abominable No-Man" get his ghastly hands on them.

The big idea is often found one degree away from where you are now. For example, the moving assembly line for putting cars together came from stumbling upon how animal carcasses were being taken apart. The success of Apple was trial-and-error. Apple overcame a series of hurdles and failures with incremental change. This enabled Apple to permanently change the way we look at personal computers, purchase music, edit video, and watch animated movies.

If you create a culture with lots of ideas then you are a Creative

Leader. A Creative Leader recognizes that ideas have unlimited power. A Creative Leader inspires the pirates, mavericks, and freethinkers in the organization to set the unreasonable power of an idea against the forces of darkness. We must all be Creative Leaders. We all can be, because ideas come from everywhere, because ideas come any time, and because ideas take flight like never before.

Surprise with the Obvious

A Creative Leader surprises with the obvious. A surprisingly obvious idea is one that's staring you in the face. It just makes sense. It springs the lock. It makes you say: "Why didn't I think of that?"

It is now obvious that people would buy single songs online from iTunes, but it wasn't obvious to the music companies. Now it's become obvious that you shouldn't need to own music to get all the music you love. Surprise!

The whole "sharing economy" is surprisingly obvious. So is the on-demand future of video that is starting to flow through our screens. Technology is the enabler, but behind each leap is someone who unlocked what makes sense.

The leap from "like" to "love" in business was staring me in the face. Lovemarks is a surprisingly obvious idea. People decide with their emotions no matter how much they rationalize. Analyze all you want. Do your research. Make your shortlist. Arrive at flawless logic. In that unbridled moment you choose a husband, a wife, a friend, a house, a car, a dog, a whatever—what happens? Reason goes out the window. Emotion decides. Love trumps. Love binds too.

Fail Fast, Learn Fast, Fix Fast

I believe in Tom Peters's credo "Test fast, fail fast, adjust fast." Creative Leaders act now and ask for permission later. They fail fast, learn fast, fix fast. This is how creativity gets airborne. Failing is just a step on the road to what works. When you find what works, that's called winning. They're not so far apart.

The important part is the fixing and learning. Without change, there is only repetition. As someone said, a genius is someone who makes the same mistake once. I learned about velocity in my first job at Mary Quant. I worked for Mary Quant for three years, opening new markets for her cosmetics line. You had to be decisive, intuitive, but most of all, fast. We had nine months to conceive, produce, launch, sell, and then discontinue a complete line. We got better at it.

Business is full of roadblocks. They slow you down or stop you in your tracks. If you see a snake in front of you, if it hisses like a snake, if it wriggles like a snake, it's a snake! What do you do next? You kill the snake! Don't have a snake meeting. Don't call in the snake management consultants. Kill the thing and keep moving.

Creative Leaders anticipate failure. They eliminate fear of failure to encourage more ideas. Spare me the perfectionists who never get it wrong or, worse still, the conservatives who never take a risk. All business is a leap of faith. Execute now, or you will be executed.

Which is better? Make 20 decisions a day and get five wrong or make three cautious ones? Make the 20. If you only make three a day you will get left behind. You'll only get two right anyway! Don't farm; hunt. Wayne Gretzky:

"You miss 100 percent of the shots you don't take."

Everyone talks about failure as a badge of success. Few pundits talk about recovery from the pain. It's never easy. It's about getting up on your feet and moving forward. When New Zealand lost to South Africa

SURPRISING WITH THE OBVIOUS: SAATCHI & SAATCHI IDEAS

Kids won't wash hands, because they can't see the germs.	Make germs visible in the form of a simple stamp. Teachers stamped the hands of their students every day as a reminder. – P&G's Safeguard
HIV prejudice, low awareness.	A men's magazine produces an edition using ink infused with HIV-positive blood (100 percent safe). – Vangardist
How to test children's eyes when optometrists are scary or far away?	Penny the Pirate children's book and mobile app, a children's story that is also an initial eye test, a warm educational experience that lets parents screen their child's vision. – OPSM Penny the Pirate
Sell more air conditioners.	An online auction synced with the national meteorological service that ends when the temperature hits 40°C. – BGH air conditioners
Bring Israelis and Palestinians closer together.	Could you hurt someone who has your blood running through their veins? Winning idea of the "Impossible Brief" global challenge from Jean-Christophe Royer of BETC Paris, inspiring the Blood Relations project, a unifying initiative through the shared act of giving blood.

in the final of the 1995 Rugby World Cup, I was COO of Lion Nathan, brewer of Steinlager beer, sponsor of the All Blacks. It was that historic moment in Johannesburg when Nelson Mandela wore a Springboks rugby shirt and cap.

I went into the Ellis Park changing sheds after the game and spoke to the All Blacks. I just said, well, you lost, so you'll just have to win next year instead. They did. In 1996, the All Blacks won the test series in South Africa 2-1, winning a series in South Africa for the first time.

Karl Smith, author, speaker, and founder of Business Networking South Africa Cape Town, offers seven steps to starting over after failure. It's sound advice:

- Accept responsibility for your own failure
- Recognize when you haven't succeeded
- Make sure the pieces from your failure have been sufficiently picked up
- Remind yourself of your past successes
- Make a decision
- Forget the past and focus on the future
- Revisit your vision.

Fail fast, learn fast, fix fast. A good game is a fast game.

SHOTS 41—44

179

CHAPTER — 12
GETTING INTO FLOW

A happy team is a winning team. Happiness happens in Flow. The architect of Flow is Professor Mihaly Csikszentmihalyi, a top researcher in positive psychology at Claremont Graduate University.

In his book *Flow: The Psychology of Optimal Experience,* Csikszentmihalyi says: "…the best moments in our lives are not the passive, receptive, relaxing times…The best moments usually occur when a person's body or mind is stretched to its limits in a voluntary effort to accomplish something difficult and worthwhile." Mihaly is the Vince Lombardi of academia.

Most people, at some time, experience being "in the zone." That's Flow. You feel unbeatable. A sense of control over actions, extraordinary awareness, confidence, and power takes place. Flow, as Csikszentmihalyi describes it, is mastering your own destiny, the feeling we have when we are fully alive. In an interview with *Wired* magazine, Csikszentmihalyi described Flow as: "Being completely involved in an activity for its own sake. The ego falls away. Time flies. Every action, movement, and thought follows inevitably from the previous one, like playing jazz. Your whole being is involved, and you're using your skills to the utmost."

Flow can happen in all kinds of spaces: homes and offices, basements and studios, stages and screens, fields and arenas. Sports dynasties depend on Flow. Spanish football. U.S. Olympic swimming. New Zealand rugby. The Golden Age of Hollywood was a Flow zone, a creative production model that drove writers, directors, and actors toward Peak Performance. Actors whom I've seen in Flow include Al Pacino in *Danny Collins,* Russell Crowe in *Gladiator,* Kenneth Branagh in *Macbeth.*

Flow is a subject of ongoing research. Good. Flow attacks chaos. The everyday melee in a crazy world is like being an elite footballer, a critical care doctor, Jack Bauer in *24,* or a pilot hitting clear air

10 FLOW STATE CONDITIONS IDENTIFIED BY MIHALY CSIKSZENTMIHALYI

Clear goals: expectations and rules are discernible and goals are attainable and align appropriately with one's skill set and abilities. Moreover, the challenge level and skill level should both be high. [1]

Concentration: a high degree of concentration on a limited field of attention. [2]

A loss of the feeling of self-consciousness: the merging of action and awareness. [3]

Distorted sense of time: one's subjective experience of time is altered. [4]

Direct and immediate feedback: successes and failures are apparent, so behavior can be adjusted as needed. [5]

Balance between ability level and challenge: the activity is neither too easy nor too difficult. [6]

A sense of personal control over the situation. [7]

The activity is intrinsically rewarding, so action is effortlessness. [8]

A lack of awareness of bodily needs. [9]

Absorption: narrowing of awareness down to the activity itself. [10]

(Not all are needed for Flow to be experienced.)

Forbes.com, "Flow States: Answers To The Three Most Common Questions About Optimal Performance," by Steven Kotler, February 9, 2014.

turbulence. Nothing prepares you for the intensity. Everything changes in a moment. Training counts, but you must "play what's in front of you."

Brian Ashton, rugby coach, talks about "outcome-based coaching." Coaching is not pre-planned. You don't coach tactics or skills. You coach outcomes. Coaching is the result of what happens in the moment. Coaches and players leap together into unknown territory.

Coaches need to get players to instinctively attack. In rugby union, it's how you handle turnover ball. The English instinctively kick it. New Zealand will run it. This is how I look at Flow. Flow is about creating an environment where you instinctively attack and go forward. You don't contemplate, rationalize, or strategize. You flow. There is no overthinking, second guessing, or judgment of your actions. Positivity is supreme. Attack is instinctive. Execution is a blur. Sun Tzu: "Let your plans be dark and impenetrable as night, and when you move, fall like a thunderbolt."

Flow is experiencing magic in the moment. In organizations, it is about focusing passionate energy, together, every day, on purpose-driving activities. By increasing the amount of time that people are in Flow, organizations energize dramatic increases in productivity, creativity, and performance. Peak Flow is that phenomenon when everyone is in Flow together. The group becomes unstoppable.

Passion

Passion gives you enough emotional equity to get in the fight zone, to optimize outcomes. In a winning company, people feel passionate commitment to the purpose of the organization. Passion is desire to succeed. Passion is desire to learn and develop new skills. Opportunities for learning and achievement should abound.

Find emotional, passionate people who love life. Let them choose their assignments. Give them an open road. Set a deadline. Director of *The Godfather* Francis Ford Coppola: "If you love something, you'll bring so much of yourself to it that it will create your future."

SHOTS 45—48

Hire believers. Crush cynics. Negativity interrupts Flow. People with a Flow personality challenge themselves and others to exceed personal best. They find meaning even in the mundane. They find reward in pursuing the activity for its own sake. They are positive, optimistic, joyful problem solvers. They are rarely bored, and are great workers.

Harmony

Unbridled passion is a dangerous thing without harmony. This underlines the All Blacks' policy of "No Dickheads." Flow demands harmony, not lunacy. One hothead moment can cost the game. Harmony comes from a shared purpose. You can't lose that or take it for granted. Purpose must be dreamed, shared, and loved.

Harmony comes from intuitive, instinctive, and trusting relationships. People in Flow have a sense of working intuitively and in harmony with each other. Flow requires fluid and flexible organization design. It also demands rapid and transparent communication and feedback.

Rhythm

When live bands and orchestras are in Flow, everyone feels the rhythm intuitively. Everyone gets the beat. Everything stays in tune. I think of the house-shaking performances of the Rolling Stones and the Beatles, of Bruce Springsteen's E Street Band with the Big Man, Clarence Clemons. I think of one single astonishing day—January 15, 1965—when Bob Dylan recorded the final versions of "Maggie's Farm," "On the Road Again," "It's Alright Ma (I'm Only Bleeding)," "Gates of Eden," "Mr. Tambourine Man," and "It's All Over Now, Baby Blue." Dylan told Ed Bradley of *60 Minutes* decades later: "There's a magic to that, and it's not Siegfried and Roy kind of magic, you know? It's a different kind of a penetrating magic. And, you know...I did it once, and I can do other things now. But I can't do that."

RHYTHM

Individual   Organization

GETTING THE BEAT	STAYING IN TUNE
Relate everyday activities to Focus.	Provide rapid, reliable feedback.
Achieve peak performing time management.	Use continuous conversation to develop harmony.
Identify and prioritize daily goals.	Provide access to free flowing information.
Deal with the tough problems first and fast.	Educate others about your area.
Demand great logistics.	Learn about the responsibilities and aspirations of others.
Delegate.	Anticipate others' needs and actions through peripheral vision and sixth sense.
Leave space for the unexpected.	Ensure role clarity.
Make technology your slave, not your master.	Confront cynicism/ negativity immediately.

Flow requires people and organizations to be in rhythm. Usually, they aren't. In my view, organizations are in Flow 20 percent of the time. For a start, there has to be role clarity. Often there's no clear RASC structure.

Generally, people in the business world are out of Flow all the time. Technology has enslaved them. Everyone thinks technology is an enabler. I think it's a Flow breaker because we constantly do the urgent not the important. As Peter Drucker said: "There is nothing so useless as doing efficiently that which should not be done at all."

People are inept with technology, constantly multitasking, forever checking email, doing no one thing satisfactorily. Artificial intelligence is still learning. Already we are its slave.

Poor time management is another Flow breaker. Take the service sectors. Customers or clients are constantly interrupting. Suits head off to meetings like headless chickens on a wild goose chase. Meetings are too late, too long, unfocused, or unnecessary. Preparing for them ruins your entire day's Flow.

To feel Flow, get in rhythm. This is about "Just Right Challenges." These stretch our skills. They involve activities of our choice. They involve feedback in real time and feedback based on actions and outcomes, as well as opportunities to grow and do new stuff. With just enough time, just enough knowledge and just enough desire, people just do it. Surrounded by Just Right Challenges, you get incredible rhythm.

Confidence

Thoughts and emotions are energy. To get positive energy, focus on positive outcomes. Imagine a positive mental image of the future, consistent with your purpose. Positive ideas, solutions, and outcomes ensue.

For Flow you want confidence, not overconfidence. The attitude is "Mission Possible" not "Mission Accomplished."

Confidence is about feeling the thrill of the hunt, the tension, the exhilaration. It's being able to visualize victory, in tandem with a strong sense of fear, anguish, and unrest. You're unsettled, but excited. Confidence is positive energy that delivers an expectation of success tempered with determination to ensure success is delivered. It's about living your life in 3D…Discipline. Desire. Determination.

Sustaining Flow

Peak performing people are in Flow more than other people. Instigators need to be in Flow all the time. The majority of people spend no more than 20 percent of their work lives in Flow.

It's natural to get in Flow in crises or for short intense periods when the spotlight is on. The challenge of Peak Performance is to sustain Flow, every day. Not easy. It requires hard work and constant practice.

Flow can be trained because it's intuitive. Instinct can't be trained. My eldest daughter Nikki trained tigers for a while. She told me: "Domesticate a tiger, train the living daylights out of it for years, and you will kill most of its instincts. Not all of them. One day, it'll bite your head off." Then she moved on to gorillas!!

Intuition *can* be trained. It is one gear below instinct but about three gears above thinking. Flow potential can certainly be developed. It's about focusing people's minds, nourishing their bodies, and lifting their spirits.

In Flow, you are floating. When you are in Flow, you know it. It is not the time to stop spinning the roulette. You feel inevitable. You are in harmony with yourself, confident, and this enhances your Flow and your performance. The "Thrilla in Manila" in 1975 between Ali and Frazier for the Heavyweight Championship of the World was a fight of thunderous blows. Smokin' Joe was beating the life out of Ali but you felt that the beauty and the joy would come through the Flow zone of Ali.

Flow is about personal and organizational mastery. You are in an environment of harmony, in a state of passion, where you have the rhythm and confidence to *attack*.

SHOTS 45—48

CHAPTER — 13

PEAK PERFORMANCE THROUGH MENTAL TOUGHNESS

Great leaders are pressure-resistant. They are mentally tough. Mental toughness means always finding a way to win. You need mental toughness for Peak Performance. Vince Lombardi said: "Winning is not a sometime thing; it's an all the time thing. You don't win once in a while; you don't do things right once in a while; you do them right all of the time. Winning is a habit. Unfortunately, so is losing."

Mental toughness is trainable. It's learnable. The reason we are not mentally tough is that we are weak. We need to be liked, or we are insecure, or we worry too much, or we care too much. We hide behind all this stuff. But that's useless. If you want happiness, to make a difference in life, to win, you better be mentally tough. You better be decisive, you better make judgments, you better make calls, and you better not look back on them.

Leaders don't contemplate, they execute. Leaders act, and "ready, fire, aim" is a beautiful thing. People think "fire" is the key part in rapid execution. Firing is not the important part. It's the getting ready and the aiming after you've taken the shot that matters. That is mental toughness. It's your preparation and adjustment that count. Be heavy on execution, and don't reflect. Use your intuition, feel the rhythm, the mood, course correct, go again.

Being metronomic about ruthlessness is a reason that the New Zealand All Blacks win more rugby games than other teams. The All Blacks are always ready to fire. They adjust. It's said they come dressed in mourning for their opponents.

In November 2013 in Dublin, New Zealand needed to beat Ireland

SHOTS 49—52

to be the first team in the professional era from the top tier to win every Test in a calendar year. The Irish had never beaten the All Blacks. After 18 minutes, the visitors were down 19 points. At half time, the visitors were down 15 points. With 80 minutes up on the clock, in the red, the visitors were down five points. For the mentally tough, this could be anytime in the game. It could be training day, because no one wavers. Run the phases. Do the basics faultlessly. Sweep in. Draw level with a try. Above all, believe.

At the death, the All Blacks fly-half Aaron Cruden missed the conversion that would have won the game. But the Irish players charged the kick too early. A second chance, a cool head, over. Gallant Ireland was defeated by the coolest of heads. As American baseball legend Yogi Berra famously said: "It ain't over 'til it's over." And if it is, go again. Actor Ian McShane's *Deadwood* character, Al Swearengen: "Pain or damage don't end the world. Or despair, or beatings. The world ends when you're dead. Until then, you got more punishment in store. Stand it like a man...and give some back."

The crazier life gets, the more mentally tough we must be. Here's how to harden up.

Change the Rules

"Know the rules well, so you can break them effectively." This wisdom has been attributed to the Dalai Lama. I'm a serial rule breaker. The more I've infringed, the more success I've had. The trick is to break the idiotic rules. "To live outside the law, you must be honest," sang Bob Dylan. There are limits, and as a young outlaw I crossed some hard boundaries. Fortunately, some great mentors set me straight.

The Holy Grail is to change the rules. Then go do what you want. "Change the rules" means get to the future first. It means reset, reframe, reinvent. The key is to change the rules before it's too late. This is crucial in high-speed times. Reset yourself today, or wake up tomorrow irrelevant, invisible, or redundant.

"Change the rules" is the radical part of mental toughness. The Chairman of Toyota, Hiroshi Okuda, told me in 2001: "Kevin, I am not at all satisfied with the current Toyota I see in front of me. Toyota doesn't need to change itself—it needs to overthrow itself."

William Webb Ellis changed the rules in 1823 when he caught the ball in a football game and ran with it; or so the story goes. Rugby football was born, the game they play in heaven. Dick Fosbury reset the high jump in the 1960s with the Flop.

An advanced example of "change the rules" is *Blue Ocean Strategy: How to Create Uncontested Market Space and Make the Competition Irrelevant* by W. Chan Kim and Renée Mauborgne. It's about redrawing industry boundaries to win in an untapped market space instead of competing in a crowded "red ocean" space.

To break the value/cost trade-off, the book applies "The Four Actions Framework" questions which are activated on "The Eliminate-Reduce-Raise-Create Grid." The questions ask: which industry factors should be eliminated, reduced, and raised? And which new factors should be created?

A key case study in Blue Ocean Strategy is Cirque du Soleil which changed the rules of the circus. It combined theater and circus strategically, spectacularly. Cirque du Soleil kept the best. It downgraded the rest, which was costly stuff. It attracted a new audience, one willing to pay much more.

When people bring me their "Blue Ocean," it is usually incremental not transformational. They've been smoking pot in the "Create" zone where they—mistakenly—think all the value is created. They haven't changed the rules. If you apply Blue Ocean strategy there are many questions to ask. I ask two. The first: why are the elephants still here?

In reimagining the circus, Guy Laliberté got rid of the animals at the get-go. If you haven't eliminated the elephant, you've eliminated nothing. People eliminate stuff that doesn't matter: a layer, a brand, an office, a meeting. Laliberté got rid of circus animals altogether. That's about all the circus had. That's elimination.

Steve Jobs hunted elephants. He eliminated the mouse, the computer tower, wires, the compact disc, the record store. He turned presence into absence. Blue Ocean strategy aside, every office, every department, every business, everybody should eliminate as a monthly exercise. Business is full of complexity. The human mind is full of simplicity. Keep eliminating. Remove complexity. You will create joy and ignite demand.

The second question I ask Blue Ocean creators is: Where's the $100 ticket? Before Cirque du Soleil, a circus ticket cost a few dollars. Circus of the Sun created awesomeness and priced it in the clouds. They created multiple productions. So you want to see more. A hundred dollar ticket turns into a thousand dollar ticket. Business people are scared to increase prices even 1 percent. Laliberté would have said: "Yeah, the animals are gone, $100 to see us."

The Last Detail

Reinvention is at the start of mental toughness. Perfection is at the end, the commitment to get every last detail right. This takes true grit, and it is rewarding. "'That was perfect,' he said in a totally satisfied voice." These words are on a photograph by artist Ronnie van Hout that I share with a creative partner. It shows an astronaut standing on the moon looking out beyond the lunar horizon.

There's a time to see the big picture and a time to be granular. A leader penetrates to the micro-level of the business. A leader gives unremitting attention to the last detail. When winning margins are narrow, the smallest details are everything. I reject the management orthodoxy that leaders should not micromanage. The caveat is that leaders need to be choiceful about what to delegate and stand clear of, and what to dive into. The last detail matters as much as the big transformational idea. The last detail leads you to the next big question, stimulating more exploration, creativity, and discovery.

ELIMINATE-REDUCE-RAISE-CREATE GRID: THE CASE OF CIRQUE DU SOLEIL

ELIMINATE

Star performers

Animal shows

Aisle concession sales

Multiple show arenas

RAISE

Price

Unique venue

REDUCE

Fun and humor

Thrill and danger

CREATE

Theme

Refined environment

Multiple productions

Artistic music and dance

Blue Ocean Strategy, Expanded Edition: How to Create Uncontested Market Space and Make the Competition Irrelevant by W. Chan Kim and Renée Mauborgne.

SHOTS 49—52

Team New Zealand won back-to-back America's Cups in 1995 and 2000. They were led by Peter Blake, a great man, an inspirational leader. Peter Blake drove the big transformational idea and the last detail. Leaders drive both. Before Peter Blake won the America's Cup with Team New Zealand skippered by Russell Coutts, he won the Whitbread Round the World Race as skipper. The Southern Ocean is a hell zone. To win that race, in the middle of a storm, you go down to the bilge, you lift the floorboards, sponge out liters of water, put the boards back. A few kilos lighter mean a few meters faster. So, you go down, and do it again, and again.

Expect to lose if every team member won't commit to getting every last detail right. This commitment is mental toughness. It comes from a sense of individual responsibility, not external control. Be very afraid if that's missing. Know that every detail of every process, however small, could impact winning. For Team New Zealand, that included Peter Blake's "lucky red socks," a gift from his wife Pippa that became a national movement among the team's multitude of fans. Personal tics, obsessiveness, it all matters. Whether it's a ritual, a sprinkle of superstition or a bucket of spit and polish, attention to detail can decide everything.

In New Zealand's 2003 America's Cup against Switzerland's Alinghi, NZL 82's mast snapped in the fourth race. You can't sail with a broken mast. You also can't sail without a boat. In the 1995 challenger series, One Australia broke in half. It sank, gone in 100 seconds. God is in the details.

Blue Heads

Grant Fox is a World Cup-winning All Blacks champion fly-half and All Blacks selector. "Foxy" was a rugby-goal scoring machine. No one has ever scored more points than Grant Fox in one Rugby Union World Cup tournament. He told me in 1991 that the key to winning test matches was to have "fire in the belly, ice in the mind."

In elite contests, mental edge decides. The winner has ice in the mind. Rugby Test titans—captains like Sean Fitzpatrick, John Eales, Martin Johnson, François Pienaar, and Richie McCaw—have cerebral steel. Without it, even the thickest legs can turn to jelly. The All Blacks' pre-game Haka ritual shocks, awes, and crushes the mentally weak. With the right focus, it can win a game before it starts.

Mental toughness is about clear thinking under pressure. The All Blacks were mentally weak at some World Cups, coming good again as the 2011 champions. Mental skills coach Gilbert Enoka made them tough. In *Legacy: What the All Blacks Can Teach Us About the Business of Life. 15 Lessons In Leadership*, author James Kerr delves into this.

It's about "Blue Head" and "Red Head." Enoka sourced this methodology from Gazing Performance Systems, a business that helps organizations improve performance. As pressure ramps up, the heat builds and our thinking shuts down. We have a red head. We are flustered, out of the moment, a runaway train. The goal is to control attention, stay in the moment, remain on task, decide well, and execute.

Leaders use techniques to stay blue-headed under pressure. Gazing Performance Systems training involves a "skill ladder," where pressure builds gradually and you adapt. The All Blacks train to win. They practice under pressure. They use switches—sayings and doings—to stay in the present and do the business.

To lead in a turbulent world, don't lose your hair. Keep a blue head. James Kerr's *Legacy* points the way. Find techniques that work for you.

The C's and the P's

Mental toughness has been researched and modeled. The International Rugby Academy of New Zealand (IRANZ), where I was a founder-director, describes it as: "The ability to perform at your maximum every time you play." IRANZ was set up by All Blacks great Murray Mexted, and

Mex underscores the need for coaches to manage minds right up front.

Vince Lombardi described mental toughness as "character in action." The model I use for top leaders combines personal capacity and capability; defining mental toughness as the natural or developed psychological edge that enables you to cope better than your competitors. In short, it is always finding a way to win.

It is about being superior in performance levels and outcomes through consistency in focus, determination, resilience, confidence, and control under pressure.

For a team to be truly mentally tough they must share a real tangible goal, and be clear, resolute, and unshakeable in their purpose and direction.

Culture is the glue in the fray. For example, every All Black on the rugby paddock knows how their teammates will respond personally under the hammer. They trust themselves and each other. Leadership has been devolved to the players. Break the code, and you face your teammates, not the coaches.

Mental toughness is a combination of mental capacity (five C's) and toughness capability (five P's). Here is the breakdown:

- CONFIDENCE Self-belief based on prior achievement, knowledge, and clarity of personal purpose.
- CONCENTRATION Shutting out distractions in favor of focusing on the immediate task; and avoidance of negative thinking or negative self-talk.
- COMPOSURE Remaining calm and focused when handling pressure.
- CONTROL Emotional mastery that enables clarity of thought and action.
- COMPLETION Envisage the final successful act of performance.
- PRACTICE A systematic pre-performance routine of listening, learning, and executing skills/drills that meld with the desired state of mind.

- PRECISION Recognizing and visualizing the necessary detailed steps required to perform at peak.
- PROBLEM SOLVING Systematic adoption of affirmative coping strategies using practical knowledge and mental imagery.
- POSITIVE Construction of a positive mental approach and attitude to all aspects of life, savoring life's pleasures through anticipation and reminiscence.
- PERFORMER Has success systems in place while using failure as a stepping stone for future achievement.

To enhance your mental toughness, learn from the experts, practice hard, embrace change, and stay positive. Positivity is the toughest P on the park. As Colin Powell says:

"Perpetual optimism is a force multiplier."

SHOTS 49—52

CHAPTER — 14

GETTING THERE THROUGH SOFT POWER

President Dwight D. Eisenhower said: "Leadership is the art of getting someone else to do something you want done because he wants to do it." This sounds like soft power. Soft power is about winning through attraction, not coercion.

Soft power is a term in international politics. It was coined late last century by Harvard University professor Joseph Nye. Hard power is forceful. Soft power is credible, alluring, and seductive. Its appeal is tough to resist.

Is it better to send lawyers, guns, and money, or to offer strawberry fields forever? The answer is both. However in the screen age, "pull" trumps "push." Your mobile is a supercomputer. Everything is on screen, instantly sharable, and more malleable. Power in an open world is how you make people feel, less what you make them do.

The United States sits up at the top of the power table, with Pentagon wallop and Hollywood dazzle. Freedom, rights, openness, creativity, and the rule of law all stream soft power. At Saatchi & Saatchi New York on Manhattan's Far West Side, visitors would ask why my desk faces south. "That," I'd say, pointing down the Hudson River at the goddess of liberty holding her torch aloft. People are drawn to freedom, opportunity, and friends. A Gallup.com headline in 2013 from a global survey: "More Than 100 Million Worldwide Dream of a Life in the U.S."

To win in a crazy world, wield soft power. Nation states, companies, and institutions will live or die on their ability to inspire movements. Power is moving people to your cause.

Here are the four sources of soft power in business, and beyond.

SHOTS 53—56

HARD POWER	SOFT POWER
Military	**Integrity**
Pressure	**Culture**
Balls	**Curves**
Obliterate	**Innovate**
Noise	**Ears**
Self-love	**Tough Love**

Family

Even the best teams lose. In business, the best families don't. A family will beat a team, a tribe, an institution, a community time after time. If you feel like a family and play like a team, your organization will operate at peak performance. I learned this working at Procter & Gamble. Instead of a blame culture, it was all about driving the idea forward together.

Most people think that family is too soft as an operating idea for business. Family is the toughest operating unit out there. Families are demanding yet caring. This is what makes them special.

There are no filters. Families are both stable and chaotic. There is tension and resilience. Families constantly evolve. Families balance past, present, and future. In businesses that operate as family, people can be their best, feel secure and safe, and belong to something special. Sharing is sacrosanct. Dreams are shared in the family though sayings, feelings, belongings, and doings.

Who binds the family? My first three bosses were women. They nurtured and truly cared for me, but in a demanding way. They aced ambiguity, networked, juggled stuff, offered empathy, and gave tough love.

Family principles offer several dimensions to benefit business leadership. Family is a metaphor for the future of business.

Listening

Great leaders shut up and listen. There's stuff on this everywhere, but the immortal Tom Peters has it down with one story. In his book *The Little Big Things: 163 Ways to Pursue EXCELLENCE,* Tom asks: "Are You an 18-Second Manager?"

Tom draws from Dr. Jerome Groopman at Harvard Medical School whose books include *How Doctors Think.* Tom underlines Groopman's point that the best source of evidence of the patient's problem is *the patient.* He underscores research Groopman points to that says doctors interrupt patients, on average, *18 seconds* after the patient starts talking.

SHOTS 53—56

And Tom bets a whole a lot of beer "that there are, per capita, as many '18-second interrupters' among managers as among docs!"

Here's Tom on listening: "The single most significant strategic strength that an organization can have is not a good strategic plan, but a commitment to strategic listening on the part of every member of the organization: strategic listening to frontline employees, strategic listening to vendors, to customers."

Spot on. Most people don't listen. Some think that they're the smartest person in the room so they all want to talk. Others pour out empathy but invest zero emotional equity. As Sybil Fawlty, a character played by Prunella Scales in the BBC comedy *Fawlty Towers,* would say: "Oh, I knowwww."

Filtering noise from the actual substance is core to the art of listening. A skill I developed to endure mind-numbing meetings is sleeping with my eyes open, half-tuned in for gravitas, half-tuned out of the gobble (and grovel).

Jack Byrum and Bob Seelert were two mentors who were instrumental in my career. Jack was a Broadway actor who worked with Johnny Carson and presidents Nixon and Reagan. He taught me negotiation and presentation skills. Bob hired me to head Saatchi & Saatchi. Both have been asked: what makes Kevin successful? Both say that I listen more aggressively than anyone they've ever met.

Aggressive listening can be learned. I listen very quickly and very hard. I pay intense focused attention for short bursts of time. In those moments, my mind is a desert. It's cleared of everything except what you're saying. I decide rapidly because I'm seasoned, because I have listened aggressively, and because I have assessed very quickly.

Aggressive listening is about shortcuts based on experience, sense of purpose, and starting with the answer and working back. Present, past, and future are as one. Connect the scar tissue of your past with the future, i.e. the answer to the situation, and work back while listening hard in the moment. Everything is framed into that purpose.

NOT LISTENING	PASSIVE LISTENING	AGGRESSIVE LISTENING
Purposeless	Purposeful	Purpose-framed
Absent	Present	Past, present, future
Sleeping mind	Wandering mind	Cleared mind
Zero focus	Weak focus	Intense focus
Survive	Signal	Sense
Eyes wide shut	Eyes half open	Eyes wide open

SHOTS 53—56

Listening should involve all the senses, soaking up every sensory cue. Listen with your eyes; they are primary. Observation is visual listening.

Listeners win in a crazy world. In extremes, at the edge, you don't know what's coming at you. So you better be paying attention. As author Lee Child's character Jack Reacher says in *Gone Tomorrow:* "Look, don't see, listen, don't hear. The more you engage, the longer you survive."

Honesty

In *Foreign Policy* magazine, Joseph Nye wrote: "In today's world, information is not scarce but attention is, and attention depends on credibility. Government propaganda is rarely credible. The best propaganda is not propaganda." Hard power and hoopla tend to hang out together. Hoopla's issue is that today everyone sees it coming.

In a crazy world, don't give people more crazy. I recall the Australian rugby union team's woes in touring the Northern Hemisphere in 2005. Wallabies coach Eddie Jones after losing at Twickenham: "If you take the scrum out of the equation, we played very well." Australian journalist Mike Carlton retorted: "If you take the assassination out of the equation, the President and Mrs. Kennedy quite enjoyed their drive from Dallas to the airport."

Dishonesty is everywhere in conversations. As soon as anyone tells you "the reality is" you know they are not going to tell you the reality. They are going to tell you their reality, which is nothing like your reality or indeed the true reality. "To be honest" means either they have been lying all the rest of the time, or it's a precursor because they are really going to upset you.

Honesty is power because it wins trust and respect. Respect is the foundation of a leader. Leadership of a country, a company, a brand, a team, anything, is built off respect. Without trust, you can't lead. You can't be loved. The best way to lose a voter, customer, worker, or friend is deceit. Shave corners to win, but do what's right.

People will forgive mistakes, but not buried mistakes. Truth also turns things around. As Bob Seelert says: "When things are not going well, until you get the truth out on the table, no matter how ugly, you are not in a position to deal with it."

Bottom line, integrity prevails. Winston Churchill again: "The truth is incontrovertible. Malice may attack it and ignorance may deride it, but in the end, there it is." Ex-Wallaby, and journalist, Peter FitzSimons: "A rugby tour is like sex. When it's good it's great, and when it's bad—hey! It's still pretty good!"

Collaboration

Everyone faces enormous complexity now. Competition is tougher. Problems are bigger. Demands are higher. Life is crazier. How to win the war? Collaborate.

Specialists have roles, but connectivity and collaboration are just going to get you there faster. If you try to do it all alone, three collaborators will beat you. This is because knowledge, skills, and training are no longer prerequisites of the chosen few. They are there for everybody so you'd better harness everybody. Access the diversity ocean, spend some dough, and get the best mix of brilliance on your squad.

Don't pick a genius who can't get on with other geniuses. You'll win a few with a brilliant bozo. You won't sustain Peak Performance. None of us is as good as all of us.

Collaboration redefines boundaries. Collaboration is emotional revolution. It's Gung Ho. Rewi Alley is one of history's unsung heroes. In the late 1920s and 1930s he was the most travelled European in the Chinese interior. He was a New Zealander, a friend of China, an associate of Mao and Che Guevara. He created waves in a country where few foreigners made a splash.

Rewi Alley founded the Chinese Industrial Cooperative Association movement during the Chinese revolution. The movement was known as

"Gung Ho," meaning, "work together." A "Just Do It" for the people, an attitude that sold action. It achieved remarkable feats through the simple commitment—and imperative—to work together. He faced the problem of dealing with hundreds of thousands of unemployed and displaced factory workers in a fierce and chaotic war zone. Chinese industry was clustered around coastal ports. Militarily this was a disaster and the Japanese had exposed this, blockading and knocking out 80 percent of China's industry. Against the hard power of Japan, Alley unleashed the soft power of "work together."

The plan of Alley and his collaborators Edgar and Helen Snow was to divert production away from the coast to the inland areas and to provide jobs for fleeing refugees. Alley arrived with a suitcase and a slogan in the then-capital of China, Wuhan, to sell the idea to the Chinese government. Alley got an imperial warrant from the Chinese government to freight factories inland and to keep them producing. Alley's theory, as always concerned neither with polemics nor semantics, was simple: get the people to do it themselves and build on a group consciousness. Winners and survivors go Gung Ho.

Collaboration is everyone playing in position on the same page. There is clarity of roles, expectations, and accountabilities. There is a participative aptitude, something female leaders have over male leaders.

The more you resource, promote, and reward collaboration, the more creativity will flow. Get the right skillsets together. Lock them in a spaceship. Give them a moon to shoot for. Rocket fuel their tanks. Broadcast their touchdown. At Saatchi & Saatchi, we call this:

"One Team, One Dream; Nothing Is Impossible."

CHAPTER — 15

MOVING FROM HIGH RESPECT TO HIGH LOVE

Fear made me jump. Alan Webber—co-founder of *Fast Company* magazine—got me to the edge. The cliff was the crumbling world of brands.

As the 21st century revved up, everything was a brand. Brands were ubiquitous, their premiums washed out. Technology was breaking people out of "the persuaders'" prison. The Web and the emerging social wave were blowing up perfect media distribution systems. Digital took control from marketers and retailers, and gave it to people. After 50 years of being assaulted by marketers, consumers were liberated to block, ignore, scorn, embrace, or applaud. R.I.P. brands. Goodbye marketing. Brand building would give way to inspiring movements. A company called Apple sounded the charge.

For the CEO of a brand advertising house around year 2000, it was scary stuff. I had seen "peak brand" coming well before joining Saatchi & Saatchi in 1997. Our company's survival depended on mapping a new way forward. I parked the concept of marketing and expanded the boundaries of business. My question was intentionally provocative: "What comes after brands?" It couldn't be owned by companies or brand managers. It had to drive a premium, and inspire loyalty, as brands once did.

The answer was anathema to the freezer box of business. It came from instinct, from my bones. Brands were a rational creation, and yet people act from their hearts. They run on dreams and desires. The gear shift was that *emotion* is the business operating system. Emotion needed to be center in any exchange of value, never again on the margins. To survive and thrive, Saatchi & Saatchi needed new language to lead clients beyond rational benefits into the depths of emotional engagement.

I couldn't codify this idea immediately. Products had evolved into trademarks. Trademarks had evolved into brands. I got as far as evolving brands to "Trustmarks."

In 2000, a conversation with Alan got me to the next level. Reeling from his constructive blowback on Trustmarks, it hit me on my second bottle of Bordeaux—and all the dots connected. Love is the biggest emotion. A brand should be loved, not just trusted. Love, more than trust, sustains loyalty for life. In our lives, love is everything, the only thing. The truth is that we go through life loving others, giving love, looking for it, sharing it. No matter how hard-boiled we are, or how different we are, the most fantastic feeling is to be loved, to give love, and to share love.

The world was getting tougher, faster, and closer. The timing was good to up the ante. I was sure love had a place in business. Love makes the world go around, and so did our biggest clients—making everything from baby diapers to hybrid cars. Time to bring them together in a material world. I was sure that love-infused business could elevate people's lives.

I expected a hard sell from the beginning. At the same time that Alan Webber published his "Trust in the Future" article in *Fast Company* in August 2000, we launched Lovemarks at an international advertising conference in London. This was just after the ILOVEYOU computer worm unleashed mayhem around the world. It mainlined into people's yearning for love.

The launch of Lovemarks drew howls of outrage from the advertising agency world. The establishment was grossed out by my invocation of the L word. They were incensed. How could I bomb their universe with the blindingly obvious?

Encouraged, I began rolling love through business. The corporate world shuddered. Blood drained from C-suite faces. Men choked trying to put love in the same sentence as business. Shirt top buttons exploded. Suits headed to the exits.

I dodged a lot of flak. Momentum gathered. Something happened. Screaming through the middle came the direct voice of everyday people. Consumers got Lovemarks without explanation. Lovemarks cut across

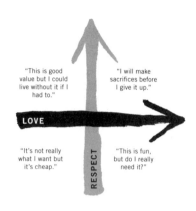

"This is good value but I could live without it if I had to."

"I will make sacrifices before I give it up."

LOVE

"It's not really what I want but it's cheap."

RESPECT

"This is fun, but do I really need it?"

cultural barriers. Everyone had a Lovemark. They wanted to share it. We set up Lovemarks.com for the harvest.

We expected stories to come in about brand heavies like Nike, McDonald's, and Coca-Cola. Instead, we got stories about everything, global to local. We got names I'd never heard or dreamed of. They came in droves, thousands of stories. Emotion's complexity unfolded endless textures of love relationships beyond family and pets. Not just love for team or country; but also for music players, women's shoes, cars, beers, soap, spreads, jeans, diapers, Bollywood movie stars—even for window treatments, chainsaws, and step ladders.

It rained Lovemarks: from Lego to Ikea, the Beatles to Neil Diamond, Shah Rukh Khan to Kajol, Vegemite to Yorkshire pudding, Melbourne to Barcelona, Monty Python to *The Hitchhiker's Guide to the Galaxy,* Superman to Charlie Chaplin, Guinness to Foster's, BookCrossing to Moleskine, Anne Geddes to Vin Diesel, *The Leaky Cauldron,* to *Where the Wild Things Are.*

This was rocket fuel. Ad agencies operate B2B, and here was Saatchi & Saatchi in the noughties building a direct relationship with consumers. The closer we got to the customer, the more Lovemarks was embraced. Small businesses got the idea straight off, and roared for more. Big business pondered as power surged around consumers.

Instead of pushing Lovemarks through, we were pulled through by the consumer. Empirical backup arrived in my wake. I hadn't waited for the research vampires. If you wait for data to catch up with an original idea, you miss the best part of the trip.

"Any man who can drive safely while kissing a pretty girl is simply not giving the kiss the attention it deserves."

— Albert Einstein

We covered the globe with Lovemarks speeches, publications, and business deals. The first Lovemarks book, now in 18 languages, was published in 2004. In 2009, Lovemarks was named one of ten "Ideas of the Decade" by *Advertising Age*. Around 25,000 Lovemarks.com stories later, big emotion has been filling a void in commerce.

To get commitment in any space, give people love. It's a surprisingly obvious thought, rare in business, but the fastest way to grow. Give people what they care about and show them you care about them, all the way, all the time. Then people make sacrifices to pay your premium. They will rave about you to others, scaling you at Internet speed. They will stick with you regardless. It's quite a thing. At Saatchi & Saatchi we call this Loyalty Beyond Reason.

Lovemarks is how to win in a high-visibility, low-fidelity future. It is a primary mission of every leader to create a Lovemark. A Lovemark is the biggest and best way to succeed. Ask your crew this: Do we want to be respected, or do we want to be respected *and* loved?

Start with the Love/Respect Axis, the complex made simple. It's a fast intuitive reality check of your position on the field. Everything of value can be intuitively positioned on here. It is the single most powerful way to show why Lovemarks matter. You can use this axis to value everything from beers, hotels, and cars to cities, countries, and presidents.

If you fail to form a relationship with your audience, you are a transaction. You are off the grid. You are going nowhere fast, unable to inspire winning loyalty. In the old days, volume and margin wrote the rules. Low Volume/High Margin = Luxury. High Volume/Low Margin = Mass. Dry formulas with no connection to the emotional reality of a connecting marketplace. Love and Respect are what define the space. There are four zones.

Commodities

Commodities have Low Respect, Low Love. From raw materials to raw deals, commodities are the lowest form of life on the grid. Consumers are ruthless, putting most stuff here as low value transactions. Here live utilities, corruption, pollution, most products, and rubbish marketing. Get out of here fast.

It's easy to fall into this swamp in an era of instant exposure. In 2015, Volkswagen crashed in with an emissions-cheating scandal. Violate people's trust, and expect to be hung, drawn, and quartered.

Fads

Fads, trends, and infatuations. This is the realm of Low Respect, High Love. This is mullet and man bun land.

It's a zone of intense affairs and short shelf lives. Think diets, snacks, toys, movies and songs, pop stars and reality shows. Last month's gotta-haves. Next month's has-beens.

This is a trial area of high-intensity gambles and quick profit cycles. In a high-speed world, leaders should be in this sandbox, throwing mud on the wall, beta-testing every day. It's fun in here, and there's money to be made, but you won't get Loyalty Beyond Reason. Most fads have too little respect to juice a long-term relationship, however profitable in the short term.

A few fads such as text messaging busted out of here and went north. Snacks, music, movies, and clothing slam the sensory buttons to get high love. Donald Trump's candidacy for president of the United States in the 2016 election began in this zone. The trick for any hairstyle is to ramp up respect to avoid a fad burnout.

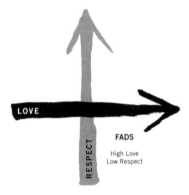

LOVE

FADS
High Love
Low Respect

RESPECT

Brands

Brands have High Respect, Low Love. They are highly respected and fixed on "er" words: cleaner, shinier, better, and bolder. Most advertising commercials hammer these words remorselessly into your brain. Brand land has become like bad wallpaper, crowded with irrelevance.

In the 1970s and 1980s—the heyday of brands—fist-pumping brand managers were kings reveling in their power. I was in the thick

of it with Gillette, PepsiCo, and Procter & Gamble, the company that invented brand management.

Brands commanded premiums through quality, performance, and trust, the hallmarks of respect. It was a hardcore rational cake. Emotional engagement and reward was an afterthought, piped on as icing.

Today, everything delivers the benefits. Everything is a brand because quality, service, availability, and operational excellence are embedded. Functional performance has been nailed and respect is a table stake. You've got to have respect, but it won't command premiums or power loyalty. Respect has been commoditized by rapid imitation, borderless competition, fast-cycling innovation, rising standards, and promiscuous consumers.

Lovemarks

High Love, High Respect is the future beyond brands. It's nirvana. This is premium territory for margin, share, and preference. The big emotion here repels attacks by price, quality, feature, and range. If you love someone, love something, love somewhere, then superior alternatives are irrelevant.

A simple test of a Lovemark is to ask what happens if it disappears? Take away a brand and people replace it. Take away a Lovemark, and you have a protest and an uprising. Thank you Jim Stengel.

The screen age is heaving with options, distractions, and recommendations. Customers play hard to get. They can easily switch. To convert and keep people, get out of your own way. Get away from reason. Work with what's fundamental. Neurologist Donald Calne: "The essential

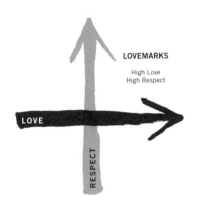

difference between emotion and reason is that emotion leads to action while reason leads to conclusions."

Rational thinking leads to conclusions, meetings and—at the point of death—management consultants. Emotion is the ignition point, the acceleration point, the only point—because in any enterprise, you want people to act.

Emotion compels action inside, outside, and across the organization. Emotion can't be commoditized. Emotion breaks the deadlock and it leaves the field standing. It has a tidal pull on the audience. It inspires people to join your movement, growing you exponentially. In the screen age, the biggest ROI is not Return On Investment. It is Return On Involvement.

How involved are people with your outlook, with your idea, with your offer? Do they want to be part of it, want it to be part of them, and all their friends? Great success flows from this.

Is your proposition lovable, constantly? It better be, because human beings think, decide, and commit with their hearts. Never take love for granted. It's easily lost. In any relationship, love has to be earned every day. Consider Nike's tour of the Love/Respect Axis. Nike started as a product out of the University of Oregon. In the 1970s Phil Knight and Bill Bowerman brought High Respect. They did it with a new name, the swoosh, a "waffle-soled" innovation, Steve Prefontaine, and great advertising. Michael Jordan infused High Love. Aspiration soared. Emotion connected. If you wore Nikes, you could be like Mike.

BRANDS	LOVEMARKS
Owned by companies	**Owned by people**
Created by respect	**Created by respect and love**
Loyalty for a reason	**Loyalty beyond reason**
Aim to be irreplaceable	**Irresistible**
Return on investment	**Return on involvement**

The *Just Do It* era. Jordan retired. The sweatshop crisis happened. Nike lost a lot of love and a lot of respect. Nike went back to its roots, it made good, and rose up once more.

Get into the High Respect, High Love zone. Stay there. Don't settle for being liked, trusted, or admired—a brand. Brands are a parity play. They met their end when power departed from manufacturers, passed through retailers, and surged around people.

The world is moving lightning fast and the audience is supreme commander. It's a mobile-first universe, a world at people's fingertips. Superior performance at a value price is another table stake. The difference now is priceless value. Not price, not value, but priceless value.

Priceless value responds to the emotional question on lips today. "How will you improve my life?" Brands have no answer to this. Brands used to be irreplaceable. Nothing is irreplaceable now. People can replace anything from anywhere. You have to be irresistible, a Lovemark.

Love creates premiums across volume, share, margin, and reputation. Love creates Loyalty Beyond Reason. How do you become a Lovemark? With the three secrets, and a modern legacy.

CHAPTER — 16

BECOMING A LOVEMARK

Business is won on relationships. The strongest relationships run on the deepest feelings. They are forged with generosity and reciprocity, anticipation and consideration, kindness, and care.

The deepest emotion is love. Love is unbeatable. You can't fake it. You can take it anywhere. To reinvent brands, I took love into business. I did this to survive brand commoditization, to recognize the power of screenagers, and to meet escalating consumer demands. The idea was to restore premiums and loyalty in a post-brand era, and make business a force for good.

Love has priceless value in a robot world run by technology, machines, algorithms, and big data. Today, producers and distributors are being cut loose by computation. Marketers are racing toward their dream of personalized one-to-one marketing. Business was never smarter, technologically speaking. But these advances are equalizers, the next table stakes; programs and information just a click away from all. They make everyone relevant, no one special.

Special is irresistible, and this magic builds through emotional connectivity. Data is essential for leaders now, but it's coming out of our ears. Name the sector, the big players all have the same data. Be done interrogating your data by morning coffee, or be dead.

Spend the rest of the day on ideas, inspiration, emotion, and connections. Irresistibility, being a Lovemark, lies in this secret mist. Big data can read the lines, but not between them. It can turn up at the perfect time, but not stop the clock. It can project patterns, but it can't blow people's minds with an idea. It can predict preferences, but it can't scorch loyalty through heartfelt empathy.

What is a Lovemark? It is an idea fueled with emotion, owned by people, and accelerated by fans. Four qualities infuse a Lovemark. You won't find this magic in any MBA curriculum.

Mystery

The unexpected, the unanticipated, and the unbelievable are priceless. It's what we don't know that draws us to a product, a person, a service, a screen, a store. This is the allure of live sport, fast fashion, romance, fantasy realms, new adventures, pop-up retailers, and music shuffles.

Brands are running on empty, too precisely defined. When we know it all, there is nothing left to surprise, excite, or delight us. Mystery draws together what gives a relationship its complexity. Mystery is the layers, textures, revelations, fun, and excitement that keep us alive. You can forget cookie cutting; people expect an entirely new cake.

Great stories are at the core of mystery. In 1996, Rolf Jensen, a futurist, said: "The highest-paid person in the first half of the next century will be the 'storyteller.' The value of products will depend on the story they tell." Since year dot, making sense of experience through narrative has been as primal to humans as seeking food, clothing, and shelter.

People need stories. We love stories. We are stories. This is why TV is the ultimate comeback kid. Classic TV has been attacked on all sides—digital to cable to social to mobile—and only returned stronger. This is because TV is just great content; and great content is the business model, storytelling on any canvas. People will always be drawn to compelling stories. If you've got a great story to tell in a compelling way, you'll have an audience—and revenue.

Technology changes how we tell stories, not what we need from them. More platforms and new competitors just pump demand for the quantity and quality of stories. They say we're in a Golden Age of TV. TV storytelling found its "A" game: hits like *The Sopranos, The Wire, Breaking Bad, Downton Abbey, Justified, Game of Thrones, Mad Men,*

House of Cards, Sherlock, True Detective, and *The Walking Dead.*

Loved brands are inevitably great stories, from the Zippo lighter to Harley-Davidson. What makes a story great? My English teacher Peter Sampson told me: "Never forget the five W's in a story: who, what, when, where, and why…ideally all in the first paragraph." Going deeper, a great story is contextual, crafted, characterful, credible, contagious, imaginative, emotional, and compellingly true.

A great advertisement nails storytelling. It makes us laugh, cry, or think. The most effective Super Bowl ads are proven to have a story at their heart, not humor or sex. The more complete the story, the higher the commercial performs in the ratings, the more people like it, and the more they want to share it. And story sharers are the new heroes. The entire purpose of communicating today is to have people share your stories.

Mystery is also about calibrating past, present, and future together to unlock favorable emotional states. Brands tend to point back (classic luxury), lean in (fast fashion), or dream forward (hybrid tech). For true power, combine all three. Let your past inform the present and shape the future.

Myths and icons weave mystery too: Mickey Mouse to Marilyn Monroe, the Swoosh to Nelson Mandela, the VW Beetle to the Sydney Opera House, the telephone box to Concorde. I loved Concorde. It gave me an extra day a week. Working across New York, London, and Paris, I needed speed.

Dreams are also mystery-makers. You can deepen mystery by tapping into dreams. Harley-Davidson did it with the open road. And instill inspiration; the Olympics is the benchmark.

Sensuality

People operate on all five senses; most brands don't. By putting just two senses in motion—sight and sound—the most potent selling device in history was born: the 30-second TV commercial.

SHOTS 61—64

Sensuality is how human beings experience the world. Our senses are portals to the emotions. Sight, sound, scent, touch, taste—when all five senses are stimulated together, the results are unforgettable. Cities that seduce exhilarate the senses, Istanbul to Beirut to Rome to Tokyo.

Sensory excitement is why online shopping won't replace physical shopping this century. People love the stimulation of the real world. The idea that people are too time-squeezed to shop is rubbish. We love shopping. Retail is a heady mix of necessity, discovery, escape, adventure, and exhilaration.

The sweet spot today is ease and stimulus at different speeds we can control. Great business turns gloom to joy through sensory delight, while baking in what Leonardo da Vinci called "the urgency of doing." In 2015, I joined fast-growing home delivery service My Food Bag as Chairman. My Food Bag recognizes that people like to cook without the hassle of assembling all the ingredients. It makes weeknight cooking a cinch by delivering nutritious seasonal recipes, and quality, pre-measured, free-range ingredients to people's homes each week.

Lack of sensuality is why we hate supermarkets, but we love food and drink purveyors. It's why I work with Booths in the northwest of England. I've loved Booths since I could walk. Go diving in Mrs. Kirkham's Lancashire Cheese. See it. Smell it. Touch it. Taste it.

A Lovemark has a loveable usability. Vision is the first thing to do with sensuality. People are visual thinkers first and foremost. David Williams, a Professor of Medical Optics at the University of Rochester, is quoted as saying: "More than 50 percent of the cortex, the surface of the brain, is devoted to processing visual information."

Vision is critical as a way to interpret, think, and connect. Our brain processes images thousands of times faster than text. Visual thinking simplifies complexity. Images don't need translation. They are borderless, fast, and emotional. Emojis are a beautiful thing.

Vision is a shortcut to the truth. If you want that big breakthrough, get your ideas up on the wall. When you see the idea in front of you, patterns and progressions will emerge. The Love/Respect Axis, the blueprint of Lovemarks, began life on a napkin at an airport.

We live in a visual age where people are aesthetically adept. Marketers are a shocking exception. Look at most product packaging. Is there a prize for the most information crammed onto a box? People are drawn to beauty, mesmerized by it. Create beauty, and you will become priceless.

Sound is super sensual. Music is the universal language. We all have a soundtrack to our lives. Nothing evokes an emotional response like music. Nothing changes your mood like it, transporting you back, taking you down, and lifting you up. Most brands miss this, or just forget. Music is a sonic signature, a creativity juicer and a direct line to heads, hearts, and wallets. I'm gobsmacked why more businesses don't lead with music. When they do, they pipe in elevator music for zombies (supermarkets are a nightmare globally).

In an all-you-can-eat music era that knows your song preferences, the music opportunity is massive. A few years back, Argentine company BGH changed out the painful "beep, beep, beep" of a microwave with your favorite song. The product was launched with a limited edition of 1,000 microwaves. Gone in a week.

Taste, scent, and touch are massively underdone in business. Each converts "like" to "love," especially combined with other senses. Remember how Apple evoked taste? A billboard of brightly colored Apple Macs that simply said: "Yum!" Smart screens have ushered in a whole new tactile world as we tap, swipe, pinch, and press our way to glory. My three-year-old granddaughter's frustrated attempt to swipe the TV screen points the way. The opportunity is to fuse vision and touch in everything from store packaging to virtual reality. The physical touch opportunity is even bigger. Amidst the screens, programs, and circuits, a real touch—flesh on flesh—is priceless. It can stir up a storm.

And don't forget the almighty schnozzle. Scent is a rocket to the brain, triggering memories for inexplicable reasons. Just how sensitive is your nose? You can distinguish between one *trillion* scents say researchers at Rockefeller University and the Howard Hughes Medical Institute. That's a trillion paths to love. "Where should I apply perfume?" a young lady asked. Coco Chanel's reply: "Where you want to be kissed."

Intimacy

Intimacy is the deep burn in Lovemarks. Its emotional power is vast. Global business has rowed hard against the intimacy factor, blushing with discomfort, but the current has turned in favor of consumers in a brand flood. Emotional expectations are at a new level, people are frazzled, and loyalty is only given to the chosen few.

It's as Oprah Winfrey said: "Lots of people want to ride with you in the limo, but what you want is someone who will take the bus with you when the limo breaks down."

Intimacy wins Loyalty Beyond Reason, and intimacy means the brand in the consumer's context, not the other way round.

The secret is to put yourself in the audience's heart, not the audience at your heart. The Ritz-Carlton did this by reframing from "Please stay with us," to, "Let us stay with you." Resonance and memory matter. The Ritz-Carlton's anticipatory service is exemplified by its motto: "We are Ladies and Gentlemen serving Ladies and Gentlemen."

Most organizations do intimacy badly or wrong, or badly wrong. Intimacy is a pitch-perfect moment, a harmony of thinking and feeling.

Think about the best bars. They have unobtrusive, anticipatory service that is never noticed; tranquil lighting; and music at the right volume that is satisfying, interesting, and familiar with a hint of intrigue. The people in the bar make you feel you belong. It's that in-the-know factor of Brooklyn, now a global city icon. My No.1 bar over the years has been Bar Hemingway at The Ritz in Paris.

Intimacy comes from three factors: empathy, commitment, and passion. Empathy is the art of knowing the right thing to do for the other person. Google was not the first search engine, but when they arrived they showed such obvious empathy for the needs of people in their search for information that it became the overwhelming choice.

U2 on its 360° tour positioned the stage in the middle of a packed audience. Bono said to the audience: "We built this spaceship to *get closer to you.*" The huge concert stage had no defined front or back and was surrounded on all sides by the audience. "The band is just sitting in the palm of the audience's hand," said designer Willie Williams.

Empathy in a commercial offer is so rare it floors us when it happens. With life right in your face, empathy is everything that's missing in business. Empathy is intuitive user experience and it is resonant moments. It is anticipating needs before they are desires. It is handwritten invites, sharing time together, attentive follow-up, and laughing like best friends. And nothing beats humor for intimacy. Humor is the shortcut to the heart. Intimate connections are more important than ever. If you can get a smile in today's turbulence, you're getting somewhere.

Technology, robots, and data don't do empathy. Use them as big helpers, not your converters. Empathy turns it around. Remember that people like technology, but people really love other people.

Long-term commitment is part of intimacy. It will be tested, and certainly can falter, but love has extraordinary reserves that get a relationship through the hard times. Commitment shows we are in the relationship for the long haul. It builds value everywhere, commerce to conservation.

For me, the Earth commitment is not about greening or talking. It's every person committing to do one thing, from riding a bike to conserving water. If seven billion people committed to DOT (Do One Thing) and DAT (Do Another Thing), the impact would be exponential. It's a leadership responsibility. Lead people to do one thing they want to

SHOTS 61—64

do and give them responsibility, learning, recognition, and joy in doing it. The philosopher Daniel Dennett said it was an occupational hazard to be asked the meaning of life, so his sound bite is: "The definition of happiness is to find something bigger than yourself and dedicate the rest of your life to it."

Intimacy is also the spark of red hot passion. Is there anything more intimate than smoldering passion? Passion energizes the relationship. It makes people want to get up close and personal. It gets people involved neck deep in your cause. It lets you stay focused on what counts. I like what Mario Andretti said:

"If everything seems under control, you're just not going fast enough."

My checkered flag on any project is: "Let 'er rip!"

Legacy

"The road goes on forever and the party never ends," sang Texas singer-songwriter Robert Earl Keen. An extra love factor, tied in with mystery, is legacy. What does legacy mean for brands—young or old—in the Age of Now, in a time of short attention spans and screaming demands?

The question was studied by Saatchi & Saatchi Team One CSO Mark Miller and his rock band of experts in premium categories and aspirational consumers. The answer was that legacy is redefined if you want to survive, thrive, and endure in today's high-speed pressure cooker.

The key is to look at legacy not as something left behind but as something to bring to life. In this instant era, people are drawn to what you are doing today. History matters when it is brought to life in ways that are meaningful in the present moment.

Team One cracked open what brands must do to build a modern legacy. Become "Authors" writing a constantly evolving narrative. Attract "Assemblers" who inspire others to take the narrative forward. Create "Artifacts" that Authors equip Assemblers with—whether content, experience, or objects—to bring the narrative to life.

The method for this is a Team One story but the principle is Lovemarks to the core. To last in a crazy world, be inspiring, be involving, and bring your past forward. Then the party never ends.

Look at your own legacy from the beginning, not from the ending. Most people think about legacy when they are exiting a role. A leader thinks about legacy as something to create every day. A leader asks this question when the sun rises: what will I leave behind?

As Maximus Decimus Meridius says to his troops in *Gladiator*...

"What we echoes in

do in life eternity."

BIOGRAPHY

KEVIN ROBERTS

Kevin Roberts has an international reputation for an uncompromisingly positive and inspirational leadership style. He is Chairman of Saatchi & Saatchi, one of the world's leading creative companies, and Head Coach of Publicis Groupe, the global communications company.

Born and educated in Lancaster in the north of England, Kevin started work in the late 1960s with iconic London fashion house Mary Quant. He became a senior marketing executive for Gillette and Procter & Gamble in Europe and the Middle East. At 32, he was appointed CEO of Pepsi-Cola Middle East; and was then Pepsi's CEO in Canada. Between 1997 and 2014 he was CEO Worldwide of Saatchi & Saatchi. His business books include the groundbreaking *Lovemarks: The Future Beyond Brands*, published in 18 languages, alongside further books on the power of emotional connections in business, and peak performance in sports.

An Honorary Professor in leadership, innovation, and creativity at universities in England, Canada, and New Zealand, Kevin advises national organizations and global brands across commerce, media, and sport. He is a former director of the New Zealand Rugby Union and former Chairman of USA Rugby. In 2013, Kevin was made Companion of the New Zealand Order of Merit for services to business and the community.

Kevin is an acclaimed conference speaker in over 60 countries. One reviewer commented that "Kevin Roberts was arguably more entertaining and more informative than any other speaker, speaking about any subject, anywhere. During the hour of his speech, there was nowhere else in the world that I would have rather been than in his audience, soaking up everything he was saying." Kevin lives in New York and Carefree Arizona USA, Auckland New Zealand, where he is a citizen, and Grasmere in England's Lake District.

FURTHER READING

Taylor Branch *Parting the Waters: America in the King Years 1954-63,* New York, Simon & Schuster, 1989.

Geoff Chapple *Rewi Alley of China,* Auckland, Hodder and Stoughton, 1980.

Lee Child *Killing Floor,* New York, G.P Putnam, 1997.

Winston S. Churchill *Never Give In! The Best of Winston Churchill's Speeches,* New York, Hyperion, 2003.

Mihaly Csikszentmihalyi *Flow: The Psychology of Optimal Experience,* New York, Harper & Row, 1990.

Edward de Bono *Lateral Thinking: Creativity Step by Step,* New York, Harper & Row, 1970.

Peter Drucker *The Effective Executive: The Definitive Guide to Getting the Right Things Done,* New York, HarperBusiness Essentials, 2006.

Bob Dylan *Chronicles: Volume One,* New York, Simon & Schuster, 2004.

Roger Enrico and Jesse Kornbluth *The Other Guy Blinked: How Pepsi Won the Cola Wars,* New York, Bantam, 1986.

Joseph Heller *Catch-22,* New York Simon & Schuster, 1961.

Richard Hytner *Consiglieri: Leading From the Shadows,* London, Profile Books, 2014.

Walter Isaacson *Steve Jobs,* New York, Simon & Schuster, 2011.

James Kerr *Legacy: 15 Lessons in Leadership: What the All Blacks Can Teach Us About the Business of Life,* London, Little, Brown Book Group, 2013.

W. Chan Kim and Renée Mauborgne *Blue Ocean Strategy, Expanded Edition: How to Create Uncontested Market Space and Make the Competition Irrelevant,* Boston, Harvard Business School Press, 2015.

Alan G. Lafley and Roger Martin *Playing to Win: How Strategy Really Works,* Boston, Harvard Business Press, 2013.

Nelson Mandela *Long Walk to Freedom: The Autobiography of Nelson Mandela,* Randburg, Macdonald Purnell, 1994.

David Maraniss *When Pride Still Mattered: A Life of Vince Lombardi,* New York, Simon & Schuster, 1999.

Andy Martin *Reacher Said Nothing: Lee Child and the Making of Make Me,* New York, Bantam, 2015.

Ryan Mathews and Watts Wacker *The Deviant's Advantage: How Fringe Ideas Create Mass Markets,* New York, Crown Business, 2002.

Richie McCaw *The Real McCaw: The Autobiography,* London, Aurum Press, 2015.

Craig Pearce, Joseph Maciariello, and Hideki Yamawaki *The Drucker Difference: What the World's Greatest Management Thinker Means to Today's Business Leaders*, New York, McGraw-Hill Education, 2009.

Tom Peters *The Little Big Things: 163 Ways to Pursue EXCELLENCE*, New York, HarperStudio, 2010.

Mike Pratt, Clive Gilson, Ed Weymes and Kevin Roberts *Peak Performance: Business Lessons from the World's Top Sports Organizations*, London, Harper Collins, 2000.

Navi Radjou, Jaideep Prabhu and Simone Ahuja *Jugaad Innovation: Think Frugal, Be Flexible, Generate Breakthrough Growth*, San Francisco, Jossey-Bass, 2012.

Kevin Roberts *Lovemarks: The Future Beyond Brands*, New York, powerHouse Books, 2004.

Kevin Roberts *Sisomo: The Future On Screen: Creating Emotional Connections in the Market with Sight, Sound and Motion*, New York, powerHouse Books, 2005.

Don Miguel Ruiz *The Four Agreements: A Practical Guide to Personal Freedom*, San Rafael, Amber-Allen Publishing, 1997.

Norman Schwarzkopf and Peter Petre *It Doesn't Take a Hero: General H. Norman Schwarzkopf, the Autobiography*, New York, Bantam Books, 1992.

Bob Seelert *Start With the Answer: And Other Wisdom for Aspiring Leaders*, Hoboken, Wiley, 2009.

Brian Sheehan *Loveworks: How the World's Top Marketers Make Emotional Connections to Win in the Marketplace*, New York, powerHouse Books, 2013.

Theodore Sorensen *Let the Word Go Forth: The Speeches, Statements, and Writings of John F. Kennedy*, New York, Delacorte Press, 1988.

Alan Webber *Rules of Thumb: 52 Truths for Winning at Business Without Losing Your Self*, New York, Harper Collins, 2009.

PHOTO CREDITS

In order of appearance

Andy Warhol ....Jack Mitchel/Getty Images

Bob Dylan.. Jan Persson/Getty Images

John F. Kennedy .... Hank Walker/Getty Images

Martin Luther King Jr. ....Popperfoto/Getty Images

Muhammad Ali..The Ring Magazine/Getty Images

Nelson Mandela .... Boston Globe/Getty Images

Winston Churchill...Central Press/Getty Images

Margaret Thatcher...John Downing/Getty Images

Ernest Rutherford ....Apic/Getty Images

Albert Einstein ....Culture Club/Getty Images

Shimon Peres .... Popperfoto/Getty Images

Leonard Cohen .... Joel Saget/Getty Images

Clarence Clemons ....The Estate of David Gahr/Getty Images

Bruce Springsteen... Will Russell/Getty Images

Mary Quant .... Keystone-France/Getty Images

Vivienne Westwood .... Michael Putland/Getty Images

Twiggy .... Michael Ochs/Getty Images

Brigitte Bardot .... Phil Ramey/Corbis

Charles Saatchi .... Matthew Shave/Darling Creative

Maurice Saatchi ....Robert Wilson/Getty Images

Bob Seelert .... Russ Flatt

Maurice Lévy... Francois G. Durand/Getty Images

Daniel Dennett.. Peter Yang/AUGUST

Rowan Williams...Fiona Hanson/Press Association via AP Images

George Bernard Shaw.. Ralph Morse/Getty Images

Lee Child...Ben A. Pruchnie/Getty Images

Norman Schwarzkopf ....David Hume Kennerly/Getty Images

Colin Powell ....Cynthia Johnson/Getty Images

Russell Crowe.. Archive Photos/Getty Images

Renzo Rosso...Laura Lezza/Getty Images

Peter Drucker .... George Rose/Getty Images

Wanda Ferragamo ....David Lees/Museo Salvatore Ferragamo

A.G. Lafley .... Michele Asselin/Getty Images

Akio Toyoda .... Bloomberg/Getty Images

Steve Jobs .... Ed Kashi/Corbis

Jeff Bezos .... Jonas Fredwall Karlsson/Trunk Archive

Tom Peters .... Allison Shirreffs

Alan Webber .... courtesy of Alan Webber

Mihaly Csikszenthmihalyi .... Claremont Graduate University

Don Miguel Ruiz .... Aaron Landman

Roger Enrico .... Bloomberg/Getty Images

John Pepper .... Procter & Gamble

Herve Hummler .... Jonathan Hanson

Edward de Bono .... Mitch Jenkins/Getty Images

Theresa Gattung .... The New Zealand Herald/newspix.co.nz

Yoshio Ishizaka .... Bloomberg/Getty Images

John Key .... Hannah Peters/Getty Images

John Kirwan .... Mark Metcalfe/Getty Images

Mike Summerbee .... Evening Standard/Getty Images

Colin Bell .... Bob Thomas/Getty Images

Edmund Hillary .... Tony Bock/Getty Images

Rewi Alley .... Macmillan Brown Library/University of Canterbury

Vince Lombardi .... Vernon J. Biever Photography

Peter Blake.. AP Photo/Michael Bradley, Fotopress

Sean Fitzpatrick .... Ben Northover

Richie McCaw .... Hannah Peters/Getty Images

Brian Ashton .... David Rogers/Getty Images

Brian Lochore... Dean Treml/Getty Images

Chris Laidlaw.. Otago Daily Times

Earle Kirton... Bradley Ambrose/Getty Images

Gilbert Enoka .... Matt Lewis/Getty Images

Jonah Lomu.. Hannah Peters/Getty Images

Kirk & Spock .... (William Shatner & Leonard Nimoy)—CBS Photo Archive/Getty Images

The Lone Ranger .... (Clayton Moore)—ABC Photo Archives/Getty Images

Kevin Roberts.. Juan Carrera

INDEX

Places

64 SHOTS: LEADERSHIP IN A CRAZY WORLD

Published in the United States by powerHouse Books,
a division of powerHouse Cultural Entertainment, Inc.
37 Main Street, Brooklyn, NY 11201-1021
telephone 212.604.9074, fax 212.366.5247
e-mail: info@powerHouseBooks.com
website: www.powerHouseBooks.com

First edition, 2016

Library of Congress Control Number: 2015960593

ISBN 978-1-57687-771-5

Printed by: Toppan Leefung
Design by: Kane McPherson
Saatchi & Saatchi Design Worldwide

10 9 8 7 6 5 4 3 2 1

Printed and bound in China

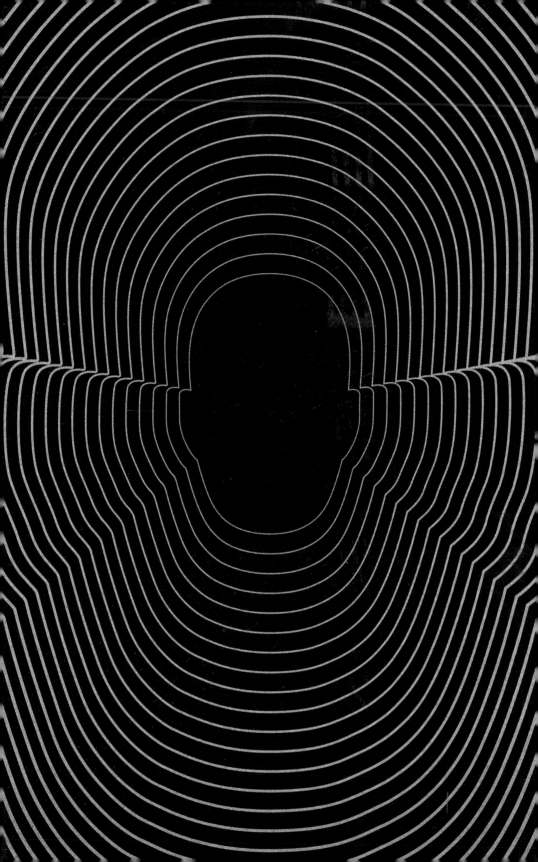